The Omicron Forex Trading Manual

By Seamus McKenna MBA

Audacity Publications

ISBN: 978-1-0684306-2-6

Printed and bound in the UK

This publication, and all material referred to in it are for educational purposes only. Neither Audacity Publications nor anybody connected with the production of this manual provides investment advice.

Forex trading carries considerable risk and for this reason you should only trade with funds you can afford to lose. Remember that leverage can allow you to put at risk more than your original stake.

Success in Forex is a function of long-term, disciplined activity. You should make risk control and capital retention techniques and practices the primary focus of your learning.

Simulated or demo account performance may not be the same as live account performance.

The Omicron Forex

Trading Manual

For Marilyn

Contents

Background

It was always probable that someone with an early background in Civil Engineering, who became interested in trading electronically, would seek to use quantitative methods to improve the trading equity curve. I also hold a qualification in Computer Science, and I have a Masters' degree in Business Administration (MBA) from Trinity College, Dublin (TCD).

I have been trading electronically since 1996. About the mid point of my career, during one of those occasional downturns in construction, I became involved in data mining and data analysis, which I practiced on a full-time basis with a number of large global corporations, one involved in fast moving consumer goods (FMCG), and well known for its toothpaste, and the other a major oil company. As you can imagine, such companies have gathered great bodies of information in their databases over time and are anxious to leverage it by analysing it and putting the results to commercial use.

The techniques for unlocking the secrets of large quantities of data include statistical methods and probability analysis, one branch of which is involved with game theory, or the mathematical study that leads to optimisation. It didn't take me long to realise that all this too could have application in my trading.

I have traded equities, index futures and options. All have their pros and cons, but the instruments I have found to be most amenable to the treatment I wanted to apply have been currency pairs, which are what is traded in Foreign Exchange, or FOREX (or simply FX) for short. The reasons for this have to do with the very large liquidity of the Forex markets, the fact that pairs have a tendency to trend more often and for longer than other traded instruments, and the effect on the markets of those who exchange currencies for commercial reasons (e.g. Japanese car manufacturers, who export a lot of their product) as opposed to the pure speculators and proprietary traders who make up much of the market in, for example, equity futures.

I have been able, for the last four years, to concentrate all my efforts on perfecting the systems that have allowed me to reach a stage where I can trade currencies with confidence and tranquillity. I have been helped along the way by the excellent books I recommend in the bibliography, such as those by Mark Douglas, Dr. Alexander Elder and others, because they deal very well with risk control and money management, which are subjects that must never, ever be forgotten, no matter how good or reliable your systems.

I have tried many Forex brokers, starting with those in the United States and then moving to Europe. They offered a variety of trading platforms. I have learned the vital importance of ensuring that your broker provides a service that includes fast execution, a reasonable spread / commission combination, no-dealing-desk execution (which means they are never on the other side of a trade – this causes terrible conflicts of interest for those brokers who are), who provide free or cheap access to large amounts of historical archived price data (for back testing and for learning the characteristics of price action), and who can supply the JForex platform, on which the automated routines are written to run. Good customer service would also be nice. The good news is that all of these things are now freely available so long as you know where to look.

The automation of parts of the system described in this manual needs elaboration: it is important to stress that it is not Forex robots that are in discussion here, or any kind of a “black box” system. They simply do not work. What the Omicron Forex automation does is to take over certain functions that are more appropriate for computers to handle. It helps to maintain discipline (computers have no emotions, and any tendency to override the system is immediately recognisable as a breakdown in the control and restraint that is essential for the working of any trading strategy). The software routines are used for extensive research and back testing. Importantly, to see automated routines in action can significantly improve the learning process.

Introduction

"I don't have time to sharpen the saw," the man says emphatically. "I'm too busy sawing".

Stephen R Covey: The 7 Habits of Highly Effective People

If you are a newcomer to Forex or even if you have been involved in trading other instruments such as equities, futures or options, you should prepare yourself using this manual or other reasonably priced resources before you part with any money for Forex training courses.

You should be very wary of web sites that promise you can make a living as a Forex trader after a short time if you do their course.

To give an example of the time and resources you might have to put into it, and the kind of outcome the professionals anticipate from Forex, consider a company that is prepared to allow people to trade from home using the company's money. They do exist. One will pay you a very respectable 70% of the profit you make. Before you can be eligible to trade with their cash, however, they naturally expect you to be able to demonstrate that you will not lose it instead of making a return with it. For this they ask that you undertake a 25 day demonstration period. There are just over 20 days in a typical trading month (5 days per week x four weeks) so this is five weeks in total. During that period they will expect you to have a 4% minimum profit, no more than a 2% intraday drawdown (the amount you lose in any given day as a percentage of the amount of your equity) and that you trade for a minimum of 20 of those 25 days. You are not allowed to hold Forex positions over the weekend (if you were trading equities for them you would not be allowed to hold positions overnight. This is to guard against gaps, which are relatively large movements in price that can occur when the market is closed and which can defeat the whole purpose of a stop-loss order).

All of these things are designed to demonstrate that you are not only profitable, but that you can maintain consistent but safe trading, day in day out. This is not easy and it is totally irresponsible of anyone to imply that you can learn to do something like this after four weeks or so of training.

Another company offers something similar but again, before they will allow you to trade with their money they require to be able to monitor a period of live trading with your own money, which they will then judge according to:

"...profit/loss (over a month), equity curve, ratio of gains/losses, largest winning/losing trades, average win/loss, ratio winning/losing trades, average time in winning/ losing trades, as well as other proprietary risk analysis parameters, which allows them to build up a risk profile" (from the company web site).

Note the emphasis on risk in all cases.

Even if you are trading your own money all the time you owe it to yourself to understand well the importance of all these measures. If you do not, you will not last long in the business.

If you are starting out, get the basics under your belt before you decide to part with your hard earned cash for training or other resources. Reading this manual just might help to minimise the number of false steps you take along the way. Then, when you are ready to become a full time Forex trader, you will do so with a sound foundation and you will not have suffered too much in the way of disillusion along the way.

Computers in trading

Every part of the trading transaction now involves the use of computers, from transmitting the order, to placing it, to keeping records and reconciling profits and losses. It was only a matter of time before the idea arose that traders could develop software that would take over some of the other tasks involved, such as putting in orders in accordance with a trading strategy. A logical extension of this is the use of automation to manage trades and so the idea of, for example, the programmed trailing stop was born and implemented.

In the large institutions this concept has been taken much further. Computers are now regularly used to operate algorithms that analyse and act on the large number of variables that can affect prices. A PhD in mathematics, physics or one of the branches of engineering can now be a passport to a lucrative career in what has become known as algorithmic, or algo for short, trading. Because computers can act very much faster than humans they can place and close trades rapidly. This has given rise to what is known as High Frequency Trading (HFT). This has been blamed by many for the large and rapid price movements that can sometimes occur, often for no apparent reason, although this type of thing is, at present at least, more likely to happen on the equity or index markets than in Forex.

Even though work proceeds apace on developing trading software, and even though other “robots”, for example those for playing chess (discussed in chapter twelve) , have become more and more effective, it would be naïve in the extreme to start one up each Monday, let it run unattended through the week and then expect to have consistent profits every Friday. Although chess computers are now almost unbeatable by even the best humans the analogy between chess and the Forex market is not a good one. The designers of chess computing engines are aiming at a static target, as the rules of chess are fixed. Automated trading strategies are and will be aiming at a moving target. The advent of High Frequency Trading itself is the equivalent of inventing new chess pieces for the classic game, or of changing the number of squares on the board.

One very beneficial effect of using software in various stages of private Forex trading activity is to provide a clear understanding of the need for discipline and how it can be imposed during the trading day or week. Computers are also eminently suitable for applying probability theory, which must be a cornerstone of any successful strategy. They are very effective in back-testing, the process of trying out trading strategies using data going back in time, sometimes years. Computers, of course, do not experience fear or greed, those twin hazards which can bedevil not only trading in all sorts of markets but also much of the business activity that takes place in the real world.

Omicron Forex has developed software for placing and managing trades in the Java programming language using the Dukascopy Java Application Programming Interface (API) which is implemented on the JForex trading platform, also supplied by Dukascopy, among many other brokers.

Similar routines written in the MQL5 language for the MetaTrader 5 platform, from MetaQuotes Software Corporation, are available from other vendors.

Dynamic historical charts teach discipline

While static historical charts are useful, they suffer from the disadvantage of always allowing the viewer to see what happened after a particular event, such as a trade setup signal.

Using historical testing functionality such as that which is incorporated in the JForex platform or on MetaTrader, with appropriate software routines, a month of trading can be carried out in a matter of minutes. Here you can see what happens at the "hard right hand edge", using real archived data, but with each bar of whatever time period you choose completed in seconds. The viewer is also seeing the performance of the strategy that is driving the historical tester and is thus able to confirm for him or her self the necessity of allowing one trade to go to its low pre-ordained loss in order that others will be able to maximise their profit potential, when the strategy calls for it.

This advantage is on top of the ability to adjust the various parameters of the automated strategy to optimise them for maximum profits. It is also a great learning experience. It truly telescopes the process of "learning by doing", which is at the essential core of becoming a good trader.

Software routines for both the JForex and MetaTrader platforms are provided with full, step by step instructions for their use in visual recreation of historical performance under their control. They can be operated easily by even the most technologically challenged trader.

All traders must think and act like professionals

While you can certainly dabble in Forex for diversion, in order to have any expectation of making money out of it consistently it is imperative that you put yourself in the same position as the big players in regard to the fees you must pay and the technicalities of carrying out transactions. Any platform or broker that imposes excessive spreads (the difference between the price at which a currency can be bought and sold), that does not control slippage, that fails, ever, to execute a conditional order or who cannot resolve prices to five decimal places must be avoided at all costs. The good news is that these outfits can be dispensed with because there are many brokers out there who do fulfil all these requirements, and in addition have good customer support, including fast response to requests for repayment from accounts.

Chapter One: Forex trading – a market with a difference

But it was plain that an increasing number of persons were coming to the conclusion ... that they were predestined by luck, an unbeatable system, divine favour, access to inside information, or exceptional financial acumen to become rich without work.

John Kenneth Galbraith: The Great Crash 1929

If you are reading this you have come to some decision regarding the possibility of trading currencies. You might already be familiar with equities, options, indexes or even commodities, or you could be a complete beginner to trading. Whatever the case, there are a number of very important considerations to take into account before you go anywhere near a trading platform. You might have been made aware of these in the past, in which case you will definitely benefit from having them reiterated and prioritised. If they are new to you, be assured that they are absolutely essential. They are concerned with risk management, equity retention, thinking in probabilities and the psychology of trading. You will probably already have heard of the need for discipline in trading. However, like many concepts, what this feels like in practice cannot be easily transmitted to new learners.

There are various means of getting over this difficulty and you will meet some of them as you proceed through the manual.

Open all hours

Forex differs from equities and other forms of trading in a number of ways. One of the most often talked about distinctions is the fact that trading can take place on a 24 hour basis. This is because there are no central exchanges, as there are with equities and their derivatives where you have the New York Stock Exchange (NYSE), the London Stock Exchange (LSE), as well as exchanges in other centres such as Frankfurt, Wellington, Sydney and Tokyo. Equity traders tend to be attached to one or, at most, two of these and are therefore constrained to trade during the hours when they are open. With Forex, bids and offers are accumulated and matched by a global system of interlinked computer networks that take the orders, from institutions and private individuals, and continuously adjust the exchange rates according to the prices and volumes that are made available or demanded by participants. While large institutions are connected to this network directly, individuals access it through a Forex broker.

While round the clock trading is possible, in practice there are a number of factors that have to be taken into account. The institutions drive the market, because they have the financial clout to do so. As they are staffed by professionals whose working day is defined by where their office is situated, there will be a tendency for the markets to be busier when these people are at work. The two most important centres for Forex are London and North America, comprising New York and Chicago, but also to be classed as major players are the traders who operate out of Tokyo, Sydney and Frankfurt, each of which is in a different time zone. Lastly, weekends in the USA and Europe tend to be times when serious traders either relax or brush up on their research and learning. Many brokers arbitrarily close down trading over the weekends, while still allowing access to their systems for research and the checking of accounts, for this reason.

Long and short have no relevance

You buy long and you sell short. In equity trading, selling short has been difficult in the past as there has been a need to borrow shares in order to take a short position. In addition, holders of company shares who sold stock could be accused of negativity. Nobody likes that. So buying shares is often the psychologically preferred position. In fact, there are some equity funds that are prevented by their charter from selling short. These are known as long-only funds.

Forex trading is done by reference to currency pairs and, as the order in which the pair is quoted has been arbitrarily decided as being the convention, in order to standardise trading, the concept of long or short has no real meaning, certainly not as it exists with equities. If you are dealing in the EUR/USD pair, for example, a view that the Euro will strengthen against the dollar would motivate you to take a long position. If the convention had the pairs quoted the other way round, as indeed might be the case in certain of the high street Foreign Exchange offices used by tourists and other travellers, you would have been encouraged to go short. None of the technical issues that are involved in shorting equities are present in Forex.

The convention that has decided the order of Forex quotes has also decreed that the first currency in the pair is called the base currency. The second one is known as the quote currency.

A highly liquid market

The Forex market is liquid. In the major pairs, such as those involving the Euro, the US dollar and the Pound sterling, many billions are traded every day. This means that, unless a trade is attempted at a value that is very high indeed, certainly above the resources of even the wealthiest private trader, it will normally be filled without any problems. In equity trading, this is most certainly not the case. Partial fills, the necessity to call the trading desk and excessive slippage (getting your order filled at a price that is far away from that at which you requested it) are all features of equity trading that either do not exist in Forex or are very rare indeed.

Benefit from the needs of commerce and dealing direct

Except in the case of an Initial Public Offering (IPO), equity trading is a secondary market, and as such is removed from the day-to-day operations of the company that has issued the shares (share allocations and options for managers and employees apart). Forex, on the other hand, constitutes in large part a primary market - there is a regular and significant demand for currency exchange by importers, exporters, central banks and other institutions, for whom the rate is incidental at the time of the trade. These entities certainly try to eliminate exchange rate risk, mainly by hedging their exposure. They do this by buying or selling currency futures, which will ultimately impact the spot market (the spot market caters for traders who need the present moment price, as opposed to the futures price, of a commodity, in this case a currency). However, very often the international merchants need, and are prepared, to make large transactions regardless of what the exchange rate is when they do so.

The best Forex brokers are the so called electronic communications network (ECN) brokers. A genuine ECN broker will have no intermediary dealing desk, and therefore will never be on the other side of any customer's trade. They will transmit the price and volume directly to their clients via their trading platforms and send the order straight to the bank, institution or private customer that is the counterparty.

These things together are very much to the benefit of the private trader because they eliminate what might often be perceived as a conflict of interest on the part of the market maker or specialist who mediates in equity trading.

Understanding the language

Over time, various conventions have been brought into use to describe the behaviour of currency pairs and the way prices, or exchange rates, move. It is important that you become familiar with these as they are an efficient way to communicate in relation to Forex, and they will also be found when you access other commentary and literature on the subject, which is recommended. One example of this is the way price movement is sometimes described as moving in pips, rather than in fractions of whatever unit is the base currency of the pair. With the exception of those involving the Japanese Yen, the number of pips in the published rate of all currency pairs is 10,000 times the value of the exchange rate. Thus, if EUR/USD rate moves from 1.23773.3 to 1.23984, it will have moved:

	Exchange rate				Pips
To	1.23984	X	10,000	=	12398.4
From	1.23773	X	10,000	=	12377.3
					21.1

Or 21.1 pips.

The rate at which price data is delivered to the trading platform is measured in ticks. New ticks, containing updated prices for all currency pairs handled by the platform, will arrive as often as many times a second during busy periods.

Currency pair terminology

There are a number of terms that have developed over time and which form part of the idiom of currency traders. One example of this is the names given to particular currency pairs. Thus the GBP/USD rate is sometimes known as “Cable” due to the fact that this was the first pair to make use of electronic funds transfer (ETF) technology, which at that time was facilitated by a cable that ran along the floor of the Atlantic Ocean between Britain and the USA.

The Canadian one dollar coin carries the image of a bird known as a loon. Therefore traders call this the loonie, and the USD/CAD rate has come to have the same name.

The USD/NZD pair is known as the Kiwi for the same reason - the New Zealand dollar has the image of a Kiwi bird on its obverse side, and the same creature has long been associated with that country.

Trade pairs formed by the Norwegian and Swedish currencies (Krona and Kronar) and the US dollar are called “the Scandies”.

AUD/USD has been entitled the “Aussie”, for reasons that are obvious.

And the EUR/USD unit is called “the Single Currency”.

Hedging

Hedging is the practice of protecting open positions by taking another one that would tend to move in the opposite direction. Sophisticated hedgers do this by purchasing options that will compensate them at expiry if a primary position moves into a loss. They would regard the price of the option as something akin to an insurance premium.

Hedging in Forex can happen when a trader decides to take a new position that amounts to half the value of an open position when the open position has moved into profit. This method of protecting profit is an alternative to taking off half the position to get the same result. The advantages of using a hedge in this way, as opposed to simply closing half of the profitable trade, is that the hedge can be removed again (closed) were the price to go into reverse but later resume its trend in the direction of profit. Obviously this would have to happen before the original trade was stopped out by the trailing stop loss order that is always used.

Another use for hedging on the same pair in Forex is where a trader with a long term position might wish to keep it open, but attempt to take profits on short term retracements from the winning trend when these occur. This would result in simultaneously holding both long and short positions in the same currency pair.

In 2009 the National Futures Association (NFA), the body that supervises the activities of Forex brokers and others in the USA, made a rule that bans the use of hedging in Forex trading as it is described above. The wisdom of this is strongly debated. The NFA claims, apparently, that the ban was placed because some traders failed to realise that they would be liable for additional commissions if they adopted the practice. While this is true, the commissions would not be greater than if two positions were opened in different pairs, rather than in the same one. Most traders who do hedging regard each of the two trades as a separate entity, with its own stop loss and commission liability.

In any event, the practice is, as yet, fully legal and allowed outside of the USA. Therefore, all European brokers, and even the EU and British branches of US brokers, will allow their clients to hedge in Forex.

Mind the gap

In equity trading, where the various exchanges close at the end of the trading day and where no business can take place before they open up again in the morning, traders can be adversely affected by what have become known as trading gaps. This is where, for any reason, the price has moved significantly while the market was closed and therefore opens at a level that is some distance away from where it closed the previous evening. These gaps are a major problem for traders for the simple reason that they can skip over protective stop loss orders and so lead to significant losses outside of what might have been allowed for by the strategy.

With Forex, these gaps do not appear overnight because of the 24 hour nature of Forex trading. They can, and do, however, appear over weekends. Because of this you should include it in your policy never to hold a position over the weekend.

Brokers, too, do not encourage holding positions from late Friday until the following Monday. One thing they will do to get this message across is to reduce the leverage allowed on your account funds over this period. This could easily cause your leverage percentage to decrease to below what is allowed for the aggregate value of the positions you hold, leading to liquidation of some or all of your position. All in all, this is not something you want to risk.

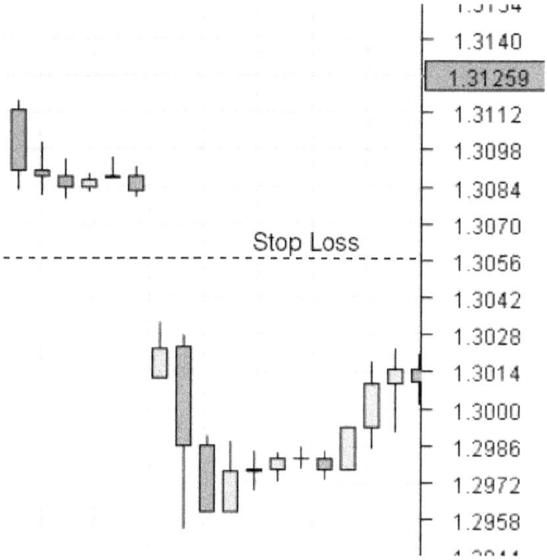

A gap that occurred between the close of business on Friday May 4th and the opening again on Monday May 6th. This would have simply jumped over a stop loss at the level shown if such an order were left open over the weekend.

Chapter Two: Automation for all traders

Has Computer Trading Made the Stock Market a "Crapshoot"?

Huffington Post headline over an
article on High Frequency Trading, 02/08/11

In the beginning there were no computers in trading. Orders were taken by brokers on behalf of their clients and acted upon by virtue of the fact that the broker had a “seat” on an exchange. This could have been a stock exchange or it could have been a commodities exchange, where the business was done by open outcry, leading to the frenzied scenes that have been immortalised in such movies as “Trading Places”. Order fulfilment was done manually too. In some cases, the order slips were simply tossed onto the trading floor when they had been filled out, to be collected and processed by backroom staff at the end of the day.

Foreign Exchange, or Forex, was a late comer to the trading scene, although the same techniques of technical analysis and algorithmic trading are now common to all. One reason for the newness of Forex trading is the fact that, up to about 1971, all major currencies adhered to some or other variation of the Gold Standard, which meant that their exchange rates with each other were fixed. It was only with the final ending of the Bretton Woods agreements that currencies were allowed to float relative to each other.

Even today, a type of Gold Standard exists. The Euro itself is an example. Here economies that were accustomed to a variable exchange rate with each other are now constrained to operate with a single currency. In fact, "single currency" is a synonym for the Euro. Not being able to allow the currency of one member state to float against the others has been a problem in certain cases, as some countries in the zone have been finding it difficult to operate their national economies without the ability to devalue their currencies relative to the economically stronger members of the zone, such as Germany, Holland and Finland. This is a particular problem for those nations that have had to accede to bailout terms from the so-called Troika of the ECB, The European Commission and the International Monetary Fund (IMF) in the wake of the Great Financial Crisis that started to make itself felt in 2008.

Even after the end of the Gold Standard, currency exchange was solely the preserve of banks and other large institutions for many years. It is only in relatively recent times that it has become possible for private citizens to carry out Forex trading on their own account. The advent of computerised dealing has been a major factor in this development.

Computerised dealing is, of course, only one part of the story. Once people have become used to the idea of having the ability to place trades from the comfort of their living rooms – something that, up to recently, could only be carried out by insiders attached to large institutions, it is natural to start wondering if there are not other things in trading that the computer can be used for as well. The answer is not only that this can be the case, but that it must be so. The reason for this is that other traders are doing it, and trading is, as always, a zero sum game. Every unit of profit that you make means a corresponding loss for another trader. It is a war and if you allow the opposition to have a technological advantage, you have lost.

One thing to bear in mind when using computers to select, place and manage trades is that the perfect strategy, whether automated or not, simply does not exist. Unfortunately there have been, in the recent past, unscrupulous and / or naïve developers who have sold so-called Forex robots on the basis that they could be set in motion and allowed to garner profits for their users without further intervention. This cannot and never will happen. It cannot, because market price movement is complex and unpredictable, and it will not because the determinants of price movement patterns are unbounded: that is to say that as soon as an infallible system ever looks like coming into being, market forces will dictate that the existing standards that govern price change will themselves change.

High Frequency Trading

In recent times the phenomenon of High Frequency Trading, or HFT, has taken hold among institutions and hedge funds. This is a controversial practice and involves the operators using computers to get themselves into the order flow of those who want to exchange large quantities of a particular currency (or equity). The high frequency trader adds on (or subtracts if dealing with a short position) a very small amount to the price and then allows the trade to proceed to its normal conclusion. The trader that placed the original order pays a small amount more for the privilege, and the high frequency trader pockets the difference. They will have programmed their computers to do this over and over, all day. The practice seems to be very similar to "front running", which was outlawed by the equity exchanges some years ago. Its proponents say it adds liquidity to trading and reduces spreads. Others have different opinions about it.

HFT has been blamed, at least partially, for the "flash crash" that took place in the equity markets on May 6th 2010, when the Dow Jones Industrial Average (DJIA) fell more than 1000 points, or over 9%, in the space of about five minutes. It seems that high frequency trader computer algorithms had gotten themselves into an unending loop after a very large conventional order was placed as a hedge against what was a falling market, which they tried to intercept. The infinite loop rapidly dropped the market without any regard for the price of the securities being traded. The situation was eventually stabilised, and now so-called circuit breakers have been introduced to try to prevent a recurrence.

The kind of algorithmic trading that Omicron Forex is concerned with, and which forms part of the subject matter of this manual, is not High Frequency Trading. It is instead a resource for traders who have come to believe that a computer can be a useful assistant in their quest for effective and efficient Forex trading.

Volatility and its consequences

Times of high volatility are normally associated with larger moves in the market than if volatility is low. Strategies that are designed for trending markets (where the price moves generally in an up or down direction for an extended period) tend to do better at times of high volatility, while those that are geared for ranging markets (where price effectively moves sideways with small oscillations) do better when it is low.

The Omicron Forex breakout strategy is designed to make its profits in trending markets, but if it is in the market at a time when there is no trend (i.e. the market is ranging), the operating parameters are set with the objective of ensuring that it at least does not suffer large losses. The ideal is to be ready for when the breakout takes place and to actually be in the market at those times, as slippage tends to become an issue if the position is taken up at the same time that price starts to move aggressively.

For the purposes of the breakout strategy, therefore, there is a distinction between two types of volatility. On the one hand there is the multi-directional type that tends to occur immediately after a market sensitive announcement, such as the US FOMC announcements on Fed Day, which can move prices both up and down dramatically in a very short time. On the other hand there is the uni-directional kind, which results in the market moving a significant distance in a relatively short time. Stay far away from trading when the first kind is likely to take place, but if possible be already in the market on the correct side when the big, one-directional move occurs. Interestingly, the breakout strategy confers a reasonable chance that the position taken will be on the right side because the large, influential and well informed institutions may well have moved in that direction a little earlier, triggering your buy on the breakout. The danger is that your position in this event will become a victim of stop hunters.

All of the above signifies the reason why you should consider intervening for the purpose of deciding on which days extreme multi-directional volatility is likely to take place, and either stay on the sidelines or set the automated routine to go into the market some hours after the event (if it is a scheduled event) has taken place.

Optimising the strategies

Computers are now used for all of the following: for record keeping, to assist learning, to allow for the optimisation of strategies and to uncover other useful information from the data archives through historical and comparative analysis.

As far as the parameters for the Omicron Forex breakout strategy are concerned, two classes are recognised. One is described as "Macro" and the other, naturally enough, as being in the "Micro" class.

The three Micro parameters are (1) the "reach" of the setup, or the distance between the extremes of the breakout channel, (2) the handle size of the trailing stop (the distance price has to travel before the trailing stop starts to operate) and (3) the value of the trailing stop step once it has started in action. The most important Macro parameters are the decisions that are made about which days to refrain from trading and the 30-minute bar that constitutes the trigger for the trade setup. The decision about the percentage of equity to put at risk and the pairs that are used in order to achieve a measure of diversification would also fall into this category.

Whichever kind of parameter is being dealt with, one thing is sure: its value is not chosen at random or as the result of guesswork, gut-feeling or instinct. It is arrived at as the consequence of careful quantitative analysis of the data.

The following is an example of how the values of the three Micro parameters might be arrived at. The pair used is the EUR/USD.

The first thing to be aware of is that the value of any one parameter is of considerably less importance than the effect on performance of the combined values of all parameters. This makes optimisation difficult because when testing, it is important not to change more than one variable at a time. Of paramount importance is the need to make a note of the values used at each iteration, or individual test. The potential for confusion is high. The upside of this is that as testing proceeds, the tester gets a much greater feel for how the particular pair under scrutiny behaves. And each one seems to have its own characteristics. Back-testing in visual mode, with whatever bar that is chosen (30-minute, hourly or whatever) formed before the tester's eyes but with the process greatly speeded up, is a powerful means of seeing the big picture with regard to how price behaves over time. The value of this is enormous.

You must always, but always, be on guard against what might be termed "curve-fitting", or subconsciously choosing values of parameters that satisfy short term or specific criteria while forgetting or neglecting the fact that the optimised system has to perform well under any and all circumstances.

Proceed by testing the breakout strategy as applied to the EUR/USD during a particular month. Remember that it is not a universal Forex robot that is in prospect here, and it has already been decided that intervention is allowed to stop trading during those periods that are known to have a high probability of showing extreme bi-directional volatility.

The month of August 2012 has been picked to demonstrate the process.

Initial values

The initial values of the three parameters are:

Reach (width of breakout channel): 10
Training stop handle: 2.5
Trailing stop step: 3

These are raw numbers that are used by the algorithm to define the various parameters. They do not represent pips, although the "Reach" figure might approximate to pips. In some cases the parameters are divisors, as in the case of the trailing stop step. This simply means that the larger the parameter, the smaller the step. Another thing about the reach is that in the case of large bars, it is the bar itself that defines the value. This is justified on the basis that large bars are most often followed by other large bars, particularly at session starts.

Conditional orders in place after being triggered by the 13:00 GMT bar on the EUR/USD pair.

The "Reach" is as indicated. The trailing stop "handle" starts out as the distance between the entry price and the stop loss level, but may change under program control as the trade progresses. The trailing stop step is simply the amount of each increment that the stop is moved in the direction of profitability as a successful trade progresses.

Label	Direction	Open price	Close price	P&L percent	Open date	Wins	Total trades
euus0	BUY	1.23249	1.23085	-0.84%	01/08/2012 14:04	0	1
euus1	SELL	1.229868	1.2253	2.34%	01/08/2012 14:16	1	1
euus2	BUY	1.22257	1.21894	-0.85%	02/08/2012 14:00	0	1
euus3	SELL	1.216646	1.22025	-0.84%	02/08/2012 14:55	0	1
euus4	BUY	1.2311	1.23691	1.00%	03/08/2012 13:45	1	1
euus11	SELL	1.23747	1.23899	-0.84%	06/08/2012 13:33	0	1
euus10	BUY	1.23995	1.2384	-0.86%	06/08/2012 13:40	0	1
euus13	SELL	1.241056	1.2371	1.60%	07/08/2012 18:13	1	1
euus14	BUY	1.23138	1.22935	-0.80%	09/08/2012 14:39	0	1
euus15	SELL	1.22788	1.2301	-0.87%	09/08/2012 15:40	0	1
euus17	SELL	1.22455	1.2267	-0.86%	10/08/2012 13:31	0	1
euus16	BUY	1.2279	1.2293	0.56%	10/08/2012 14:15	1	1
euus22	BUY	1.23628	1.2345	-0.83%	13/08/2012 13:50	0	1
euus23	SELL	1.233506	1.2353	-0.84%	13/08/2012 15:55	0	1
euus25	SELL	1.232284	1.2306	0.58%	14/08/2012 14:33	1	1
euus26	BUY	1.234058	1.2341	0.02%	16/08/2012 14:20	1	1
euus29	SELL	1.2337	1.23215	0.65%	17/08/2012 13:38	1	1
euus34	BUY	1.232346	1.24494	5.96%	20/08/2012 13:53	1	1
euus36	BUY	1.245424	1.2537	4.65%	22/08/2012 13:42	1	1
euus38	BUY	1.25564	1.2561	0.33%	23/08/2012 14:26	1	1
euus40	BUY	1.25125	1.25313	0.98%	24/08/2012 14:01	1	1
euus47	SELL	1.251696	1.249	2.25%	27/08/2012 13:44	1	1
euus51	SELL	1.253158	1.25518	-1.02%	29/08/2012 13:54	0	1
euus53	SELL	1.253316	1.25265	0.36%	30/08/2012 14:26	1	1
euus55	SELL	1.26016	1.2602	-0.02%	31/08/2012 13:50	0	1
euus54	BUY	1.26269	1.26115	-0.92%	31/08/2012 14:19	0	1
				10.90%		13	26
		Commissions		0.61%			
			Nett	10.29%	Win rate		50.00%

The above table shows the result of the breakout strategy on EUR/USD for the full month of August 2012. The settings for the parameters have been optimised at Reach (breakout channel width): 10, Trailing stop handle: 1.25 and trailing stop step: 3. The trigger bar is 13:00 GMT 30-minute bar.

These are figures based on optimised parameters. This means that time went into testing all sorts of different combinations of the parameter values. Will the outcome be the same if the automated strategy is run next month, or in any other month you choose to select? The answer is almost certainly not. The result is not likely to be better and it could be a lot worse. It might even be a loss. The real value of the exercise lies in allowing judgements to be made about what constitutes the important factors in trading success. When you have carried out many exercises of the sort described here, you will be in little doubt but that risk control and money management are paramount. This will be mentioned often - it is one fact that can bear frequent repetition. One risk mitigator is the use of several currency pairs at once. This has been found to be of value in ironing out extremes in the equity curve. Always remember, however, that when several pairs are used the amount risked on each must be adjusted to keep within money management guidelines.

The parameters might well be readjusted in the light of results over a longer period. Quarterly is a good choice as this represents the normal reporting period for businesses and institutions. Seasonality is another factor that must be borne in mind.

It has already been seen that days of potential high volatility might be better avoided. They should be taken out and the routine run again with the same parameters and time period. But here is the thing: those days simply cannot be picked by reference to the trade log just produced. That would be curve-fitting, otherwise known as cherry picking. Whatever changes are made must be capable of getting good results in all other months. For this reason they must be specific, generic modifications that will always apply.

Profit and loss example

Below is a portfolio report on all trades that were placed on the GBP/USD pair during the month of February 2012 using the Dukascopy historical tester, which allows a software routine to be used on archived data. While this is simulated, every tick is accounted for and the results do represent an accurate assessment of what would have transpired under live conditions.

With the sole exception of the users deciding the days on which no trading should take place, the strategy criteria for choosing and managing each trade were the same throughout or were under the control of the software, without any user intervention, during the period. These included the 30 hour bar chosen as the base, or datum, for the calculation of the entry and stop loss orders, and the computations for the position size, the "handle" size for the trailing stop and the size of the trailing stop step.

Trade label		Open price	Close price		Open date	Close date
gbus0	BUY	1.5773	1.5812	2.18%	6/2/12	6/2/12
gbus2	BUY	1.5813	1.5814	0.06%	7/2/12	7/2/12
gbus5	SELL	1.5885	1.5828	3.34%	8/2/12	8/2/12
gbus7	SELL	1.5846	1.5866	-0.82%	9/2/12	9/2/12
gbus9	SELL	1.5751	1.5746	0.21%	10/2/12	10/2/12
gbus15	SELL	1.5787	1.5715	4.25%	13/2/12	14/2/12
gbus17	SELL	1.5702	1.5689	0.78%	14/2/12	14/2/12
			Total	10.00%		
			Commissions	0.21%		
			Nett	9.79%		

Back-tested strategy out turn for one month in 2012

Please note that in the example above the percentages quoted are percentages of equity in the account and do not represent the relative rise and fall of the exchange rate. The amount wagered in each trade will have been different than others.

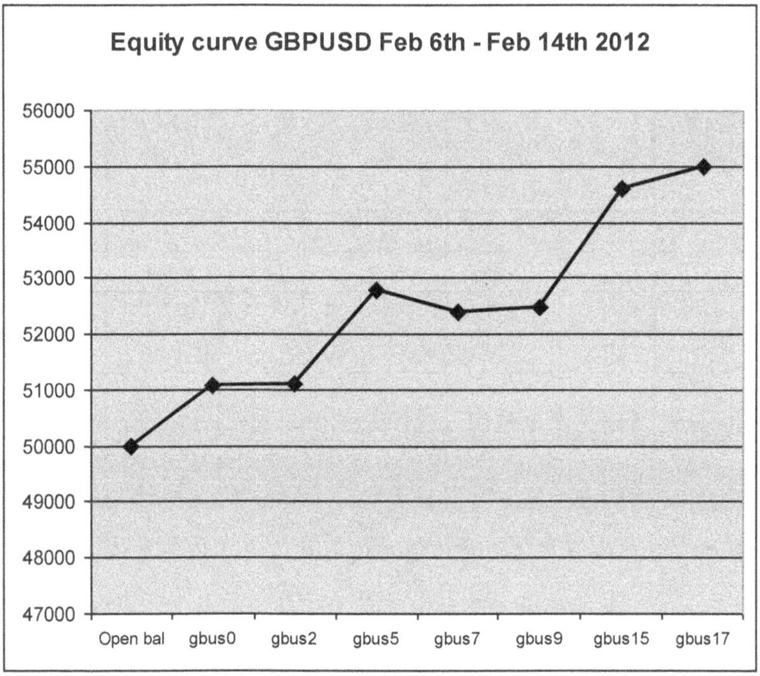
Equity curve GBPUSD Feb 6th - Feb 14th 2012
56000
55000
54000
53000
52000
51000
50000
49000
48000
47000
Open bal
gbus0
gbus2
gbus5
gbus7
gbus9
gbus15
gbus17

An extended example

Here is an example of a more extended period of trading. The equity curve below is for the EURUSD pair during the first six months of 2012.

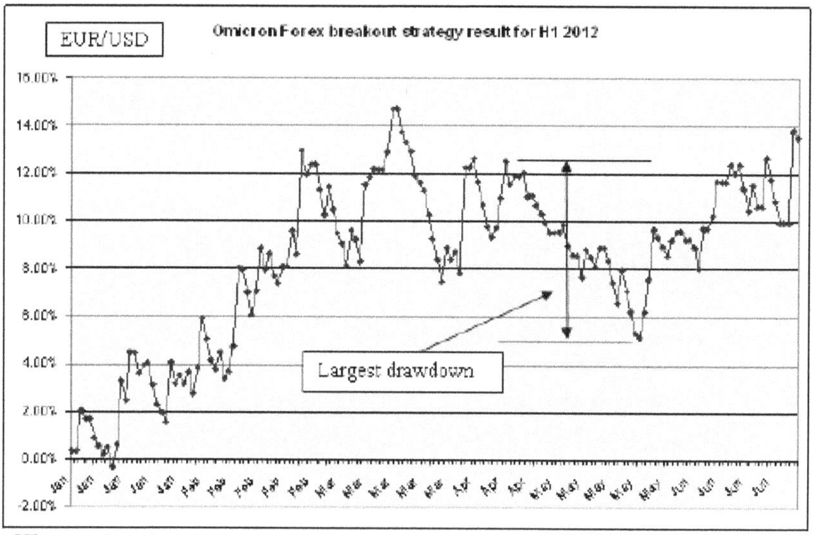

JForex historical tester Results for the Omicron Forex breakout automated strategy for the first six months of 2012

The main characteristic of the strategy was a tight Stop Loss setting under the control of the trailing stop incorporated in the strategy. The stop loss "handle", or the distance price has to go from the entry level before the trailing stop starts to operate, was made relatively very short. Trades took place every day on which trading was possible, including Fed days and US Non-Farm payroll days. These results are for one currency pair, EUR/USD.

The vital statistics are:

The vital statistics are:

Profit & Loss (gross)	13.53%
Commissions	2.18%
Net	11.35%
Win ratio	36.42%
Largest win	4.46%
Largest loss	-1.11%
Largest drawdown	7.33%

All percentages are percentages of starting equity with no withdrawals during the period

It can be seen from the graph that the May period was the one in which profitability went into reverse. This might just reflect the old adage in equity trading: “Sell in May and go away”. Perhaps the large Forex players adhere to the same principle, which would result in a thin, choppy market that would not suit a breakout strategy.

The next graph is of the same instrument over the same period, with all parameters exactly the same with the exception of the trailing stop, which has been made less tight than in the first example. The “handle” has now been increased by a factor of three. In theory this should allow trades to develop better and, indeed, the win ratio is slightly improved. The largest drawdown and the overall profitability are not as good, however.

The equity curve in the looser trailing stop example is also more volatile, showing big wins and longer periods of continuous losses as opposed to the smoother progression that is to be preferred.

One point to note though is that the maximum profit reached exceeded that of the first example. This, however, is a comment made with the benefit of hindsight.

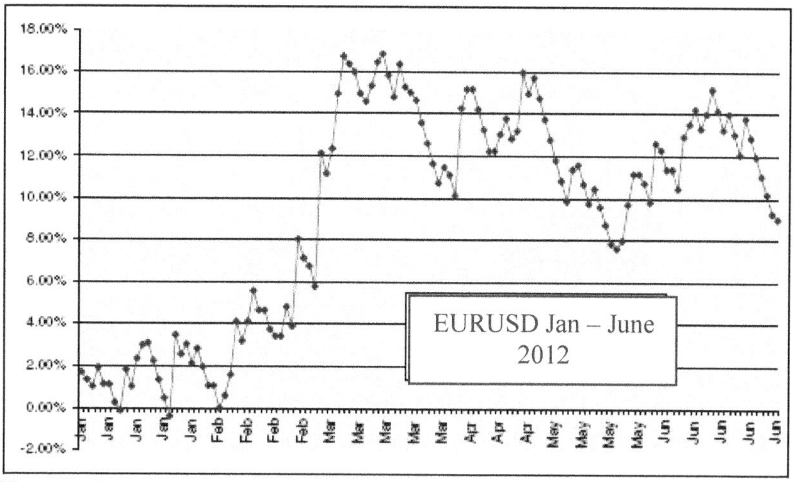

The same instrument traded over the same period as in the previous example but with a looser trailing stop.

On this occasion the relevant figures are:

Profit & Loss (gross)		9.02%
Commissions		1.71%
	Net	7.31%
Win ratio		39.68%
Largest win		6.36%
Largest loss		-1.07%
Largest drawdown		8.32%

Comparisons of this kind over significant periods can be very valuable in helping to gain an understanding of what is important in Forex trading. This example reinforces the well observed fact that control of loss and profit protection through careful trade management is vital.

Uncovering other insights

As well as the Historical Tester, the Dukascopy JForex trading platform incorporates the Historical Data Manager. This makes a large amount of historical price and time data available so that other, relevant, information can be unlocked from it. The importance of dealing in probabilities has been emphasised elsewhere. Therefore, as one example, it would make sense to uncover the best time bars on the chart from which the breakout strategy might be launched.

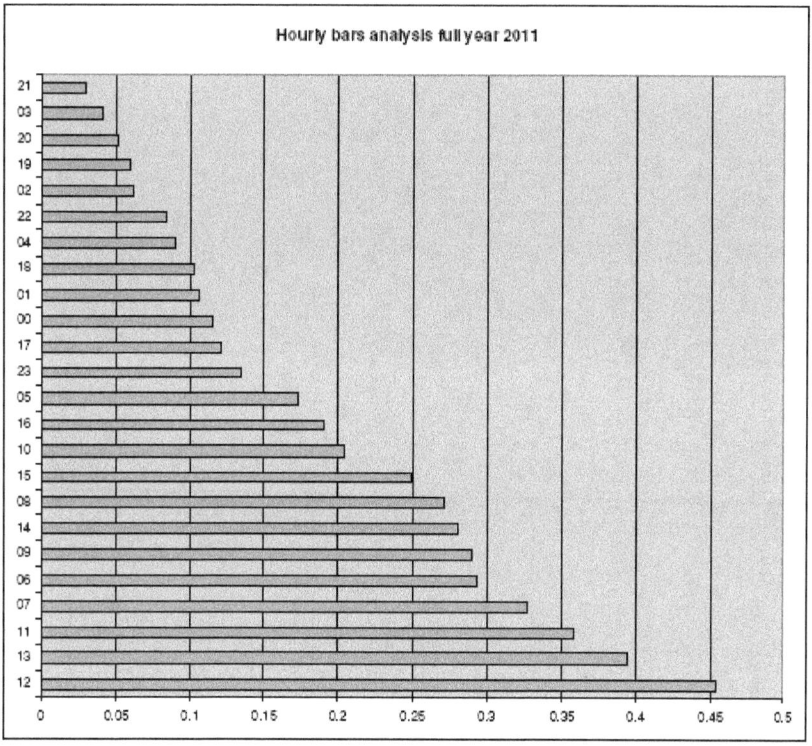

The above is an analysis, for the EURUSD pair, of the relative frequency of hourly bars over the full year of 2011 that were followed by at least two other bars going in the same direction. This is perceived to be an indication of the best time at which to initiate the Omicron Forex Breakout Strategy automated routine.

As always, the results have to be treated with caution and supported by other testing, but partly as a result of the above it was determined that the best time to initiate the strategy was at the close of the 13:00 GMT 30-minute bar. Other information was gleaned from analysis showing the results of trades that were initiated in this manner.

Chapter Three: Relevant concepts – giving yourself the best possible advantage

"A reporter once asked Albert Einstein, 'What do you consider the greatest invention of all time?' The good doctor thought only a few seconds and then replied, 'Compound interest.'

Allyson Lewis: "The Million Dollar Car and $250,000 Pizza"

The trailing stop

Given that the only sure thing in Forex is that the trade can turn around and go in the wrong direction at any time, it is of vital importance to lock in profit as soon as it is made. A number of techniques are used for this, one of the most important of which is the trailing stop.

At this stage it should be understood by all market participants that trading without the benefit of a stop loss order is sheer lunacy. It is a safety net that prevents total disaster in the event that any given trade goes in the wrong direction. Its usefulness doesn't stop there, however. It must also be used to lock in paper profits and to quickly reduce the risk of any loss at all in the trade. In order to allow it to do that it needs to be moved, as on a one-way street, in the direction of profit as soon as the exchange rate starts to go in the right direction.

The trailing stops have been automated and made an integral part of the Omicron Forex automated trading routine. Immediately a trade starts to move beyond the entry price into profit the trailing stop software starts to operate so that it can move the stop loss order in the right direction. Once again, it has been established that the trailing stop is of immense significance for the success of the trading strategy. The design of its component parts is a truly important factor in the success of the method.

A trailing stop is made up of two essential elements, the profit level at which the first move is made and the steps in profit on which any subsequent ratchet up or down takes place. The distance from the entry to the point at which the first step is triggered is called the "handle". This can be independent of the distance from the entry to the original stop loss level that was put in place when the order was initiated, although this is normally the starting position.

Below is what the sequence of events looks like when a trade has moved into profit. The trailing stop has taken control of the stop loss order, according to the programmed handle size and step amount. Care has gone into finding the optimum values for both of these. If the trailing stop is too loose excess paper profit will be given back in the event of a reversal. If it is too tight the trade will not have a chance to develop.

Trailing stop in action:

Conditional long entry with stop loss.

Order triggered – stop loss is going towards profit.

First profit level is reached. Stop loss has been trailed to better than entry level.

Even if your trade is not under the control of a software routine you should still trail the stop loss manually in order to lock in profits. Paper profits constitute part of your equity and, as such, must be fiercely protected. Stop loss orders only go in one direction, like a ratchet, towards profitability.

Compounding

If you begin trading with a certain amount in your account (your equity) and you make a profit in the first month, you will obviously have a larger amount at the start of the second month. The same percentage profit will therefore result in somewhat larger absolute earnings in the second period. This is the basis of compounding. Over time it is very powerful.

Consider the following, where the account contained 1000 units at the beginning and a profit of 4% per period was achieved each month (please note that this is a notional concept and is used here for illustration – real life is not so neat). Over twelve periods the result would be as shown below – a compounded increase of 601 units, or 60%, while the simple result of 4% multiplied by 12 only comes to 48%.

		Mth 1	Mth 2	Mth 3	Mth 4	Mth 5	Mth 6	Mth 7	Mth 8	Mth 9	Mth 10	Mth 11	Mth 12
At start of each month		1,000	1,040	1,082	1,125	1,170	1,217	1,265	1,316	1,369	1,423	1,480	1,539
Monthly increase	4%	40	42	43	45	47	49	51	53	55	57	59	62
		1,040	1,082	1,125	1,170	1,217	1,265	1,316	1,369	1,423	1,480	1,539	**1,601**

As you might expect, mathematicians have developed a formula for compound interest. It is written as:

$$A = P(1+r)^n$$

Where:

A = Amount at end of period
P = Amount at start of period (amount to be compounded, say 1000 in this example)
r = Interest rate (say 4.00%)
n= Number of periods over which compounding is to take place (say 12).

To work out the total amount at the end of the 12 periods, a spreadsheet entry would be entered like this:

= 1000 * ((1+ 0.04) ^ 12)

0.04 is another way of writing 4.00%, "*" stands for "multiplied by" and "^" means "raised to the power of".

Over many periods, consistent success can lead to impressive amounts when profits are achieved and compounded. This is one reason why percentages should be used in the calculations carried out for trading. Another, very important one is that this method also works in reverse. If you confine the amount that you risk to a percentage of your equity for each trade as opposed to using an absolute amount, and you hit a losing streak, you will progressively risk less on each new trade. This will keep you in the game longer. Just as in any other business, money is the lifeblood of trading.

Trading styles, short term or long

It is important to understand the kind of trading this manual concentrates on. While it is not exactly day trading, as positions can and often are held overnight, neither is it position or swing trading, which can often have a time frame longer than a week or more. Typically, under the Omicron Forex breakout strategy it would be expected to place around 20 trades in a month per currency pair, and often less than that.

This highlights the subject of trading styles. Different trading styles suit different personalities and, as with everything else one wishes to excel at, the trader must be comfortable with the type of trading chosen.

There are those who might be better classified as investors rather than traders. These are the people who are prepared to take a position and hold it for a long time on the basis of some principle they have adopted. While this is normally more appropriate to those who are interested in equities, it could have application in Forex too. Someone who took a view on the decline of the Euro after the news broke of the Greek sovereign debt difficulties in 2011 could have been quite successful by selling Euros and holding the position, through thick and thin, for over a year:

At the end of May 2011 the Greek crisis started a downward movement in the Euro that lasted for a full year. A EUR/USD exchange rate of 1.20 has been a natural floor for this pair for some time.

At the other end of the spectrum are the traders who are known as "scalpers". They will make a great many trades in the course of a day and be satisfied with a very small gain on each. This type of trading requires constant vigilance and nerves of steel. It is not for everyone.

The Omicron Forex breakout strategy is somewhere in the middle of the two extremes just described. When it is in operation, trades will be held for a number of hours or even overnight if they are going well. If they go badly they will be terminated somewhat sooner. The strategy thinks in probabilities and has no sentiment, no fear and no greed.

Readers of this manual must decide for themselves what their trading style is. If they require the staid progress of an investment, they need to decide that now. If they live for the adrenaline rush that scalping can bring, then so be it. If they feel that making money is about a reasonable, steady approach to learning the behaviour of currency pair price movement, combined with the kind of back testing and other research that leads to solid trading within a five day time frame, then read on.

Analysis, both fundamental and technical

In the beginning there was fundamental analysis, which started out in the equity markets. The activities of quoted companies were examined in the context of the financial and business environment in order to estimate what the share price might do in the future. Then people began to examine charts of how the price performed over time. They noticed, or claimed to notice, that patterns appeared from time to time that had predictive ability. If you have had any exposure at all to trading you will be conversant with double and triple tops and bottoms, head and shoulders patterns, flags and pennants. These still have validity, if only for the reason that so many other market participants pay attention to them - they can become self-fulfilling prophecies. Analysis of this sort is called technical analysis and it has tended to overtake fundamental analysis in terms of popularity among traders.

Trading indicators are under the heading of technical analysis. These include moving averages and such things as stochastics and moving average convergence / divergence (MACD) indicators. It must be remembered that all of these are lagging indicators.

One fundamental principle of trading has to be that it is, in fact, impossible to foretell the future. When any individual trade is placed, the trader has to take into account the very real possibility that the price will go in the opposite direction to that which is desired. This can happen many times in succession and it is the ability to deal with something like that which indicates whether or not the trader has the right psychology for trading.

Thinking in probabilities takes into account the behaviour of a large number of trades. This allows for strategies that are designed to increase the odds of more going in the right direction than might otherwise be the case, and of the aggregate value of winners being significantly greater than that of losers.

Chapter Four: Let the institutions tell you the market direction

***John Tuld**: There are three ways to make a living in this business: be first, be smarter, or cheat.*

J. C. Chandor: Margin Call (Movie)

The Forex market worldwide is very large indeed. Billions and billions of whatever currency unit you wish to consider are exchanged every day. The majority of this trade is in transactions involving what are known as the majors – the US dollar, the Euro, the Pound sterling, the Japanese Yen, the Canadian Dollar, the Australian Dollar and the Swiss Franc. Other popular trading currencies are the Scandies or the Swedish Krona and the Norwegian Kroner, and the New Zealand Dollar.

Currencies that are also traded, but to a lesser extent, include the Singapore dollar and those units that are used in the major economies of Latin America, for example the Brazilian Real. While China has become a very serious player indeed in global commerce and finance, its currency, the Remnimbi or Yuan, is at present tied to a narrow range against the US dollar by the intervention, when required for this purpose, of the Chinese monetary authorities. The Indian government discourages currency exchange in India that involves the rupee for anything other than commercial purposes.

The larger players

The largest proportion of daily Forex transactions involves the inter-bank trade - about 50%. This is not surprising, as these institutions need currency exchange for their exporting and importing commercial clients, and for customers that are tourists and other travellers. However, they also engage in Forex trading for speculative purposes on their own accounts. After the inter-bank market, institutions like insurance companies, hedge funds, and other concerns that have access to cash flow play an important part. These can include the financial arms of major manufacturers, such as car makers, who have treasury departments to assist marketing (vehicle leasing and other, related, finance) and the foreign exchange that the company may require to facilitate exports of the finished product. In this regard it should be noted that some foreign exchange is carried out, not for the purpose of making a profit, but to provide the means by which the company can operate. For example, it is well recognised that the end-of-month commercial account settling by Japanese exporters can have an effect on the Yen exchange rate. At other times currency futures are bought and sold in order to reduce exchange rate risk, which is the original hedging activity.

And then there are the private traders, many of whom, it is hoped, are reading this manual. They access the market via their brokers, and represent the most fragmented segment of the market.

As noted elsewhere, the institutional traders of one sort or another are the market movers. This is because they deal in very large amounts whenever they put on a trade. This, in reality, means that everybody else is following their lead. They employ research departments, trading teams, risk managers and strategic analysts. Their reaction to any event often seems to be the result of the most convoluted reasoning, and can also seem counterintuitive in the extreme. For all these reasons there is really not much point in attempting to second guess what they will decide to do.

Forex traders only want to be profitable

For the purposes of trading you should not be interested in what monetary policy, or any of the other things that influence the market, *should* be. You are only interested in the behaviour of currency exchange rates, period. There is nothing more incongruous than to occasionally get an email from a market analyst whose commentary consists of prescriptions for what the chairman of the Fed should do, according to the analyst, rather than taking note of what that gentleman has done and acting accordingly.

The Forex trader has to decide whether he or she is in the business of advising policy makers or of taking part in an activity that will in the long run be profitable. The two are totally incompatible.

So while the future cannot be foreseen, and therefore the direction of prices at a later time, the best attempt can at least be made to take advantage of what is happening in the present. That consists of reading what the institutions that move the market are doing and letting them show the way forward. Do not suffer from the delusion that smaller traders can either move the market themselves or anticipate the actions of the people who do move it in advance of them deciding how to place their trades. Apart from anything else, one could be forgiven for suspecting that the big players, from time to time, will assume totally irrational positions for the sole purpose of wrong footing the smaller trader. This might not be such a fanciful idea. As Andy Grove, founder member and former CEO of Intel, said in the title of one of his books: “Only the Paranoid Survive”.

Chapter Five: Risk management and capital preservation

No "safe" trading system has ever been devised, and no one can guarantee profits or freedom from loss

Zulutrade Inc. website disclaimer

Risk management and capital preservation are two separate subjects. The former includes such things as diversification and the fine-tuning of the criteria that govern strategy software routines in order to maximise the benefits to be derived from them. Capital preservation is about having limits on position sizes and a cap on the amount that can be lost each month.

Survival first

A proprietary trader, one who operates his own account or who trades with other people's money, must survive in order to prosper. Everybody who has ever been tempted to enter the world of trading, whatever the instruments to be traded, has done so on the hope and expectation of making profits. In reality, experience very quickly teaches that profits are not, in fact, the most important thing to aim for. The most important consideration in trading is the management of risk, which takes in, among other things, money management and the retention of equity.

No intervening

Novice traders live for the moment. Each trade takes on the aspect of a special event, to be watched closely and either fretted over, if it seems to be going in the wrong direction, or cheered and made to form the basis of feelings of elation if it looks like it is succeeding. Successful, properly trained and experienced traders, on the other hand, regard any individual position taken almost with indifference. If it has any claim to attention at all, it will be in order to advance learning about what might be called the anatomy of the trade. This learning might be used in the systematic, methodical modification of the overall trading strategy. Above all, successful traders will not arbitrarily intervene in the progress of the current trade. Decisions about how it is to be managed will have been made long before, during the development of the written trading plan.

In all commercial activity there are rules of thumb. These will have been developed over a long time and will have the support and agreement of the battle hardened players who are making a success of it. Thus, in property investment for example, the price paid for a building should not exceed 15 times the annual rent that is expected and it should be acquired for considerably less than that, if at all possible. So it is in trading. It is generally accepted that a risk of no more than 2% of equity should be taken on any trade. This is an absolute maximum and many institutions will not allow its traders to risk more than half that on a position. There are other rules. In the event that a losing streak is encountered, no more than 6% of equity can be lost in a month. If that level is hit, trading for the rest of the month is suspended.

Calculating position size

All Forex brokers allow for leverage. This means that a trader client can multiply his or her account value by a factor, normally between 100 and 300, in order to come to the amount that can actually be used for trading. So if you have deposited 50,000 (US dollars, Euros, Aussie dollars or whatever your local currency is), and you are allowed leverage of 100 you will, in theory, be able to place a single trade that has a value of 5,000,000 (five million or 5.00 MM according to the convention for recording large amounts), currency units. At the time of writing the EUR/USD exchange rate is 1.23655. It is not unreasonable that it will move up a cent, to 1.24655, later in the day. In the expectation that this will actually happen, 5.00 MM Euros could be bought. This would cost 6.182750 MM US dollars, or 5.00 MM multiplied by 1.23655. Later, if the view taken turns out to be correct, the original 5.00 MM Euros would then be worth 6.232750 MM dollars, giving a profit of 50,000.00. The account would have been doubled.

Now, it is also possible, and approaching a certainty in the long run, that the move on the day would be against the position. The trader's view could turn out to be wrong. All that would be required in that case to completely wipe out the account - to lose everything - would be for the change in the rate to reduce by one cent, instead of increasing by that amount. This would represent total disaster. The broker has a computer system monitoring all accounts on its books. This is programmed to close out positions where equity has reduced to below a certain figure, which will never be negative. In this case the loss is locked in. But it is the trader's loss, not the broker's. Like all other machines, the broker's computer has no emotions and is just as happy to close the trader out as it is to record a profit for him or her, should one be made. This is the danger of leverage and a clear indication that it must be used sensibly.

	Position size (EUR)	Exchange rate	Position size (USD)
At open	5,000,000.00	1.23655	6,182,750.00
At close		1.22655	6,132,750.00
	Profit and Loss (P&L)		-50,000.00*
*P&L amount will always be worse than this because of commissions, slippage and possible overnight charges			

Figure 1

Leverage effectively amounts to a loan from the broker, which is secured on the value of the client account. Like all loans, this attracts charges, including interest. Therefore, if a position is held overnight, an overnight charge will be applied on top of the commissions, which are debited at the points in time when the position is opened and closed.

What would that trade look like if the rule that says we should risk no more than 1% of equity had been applied? In order to illustrate this, another element needs to be defined: the stop loss level. This is the exchange rate at which it has been decided to recognize the loss and get out of the position, preserving equity so that the trader can "fight another day". In the above case, the strategy might define this, based on our research and in order to create the best probability of being profitable over time despite such a loss on a single trade, to be at the level of 1.23465.

Now all the information needed to define how big our position should be is known. The calculation is as follows:

Total equity at start of trade:	50,000.00
Risk of 1% of equity (risk amount)	500.00
Open rate	1.23773
Stop loss rate	1.23465
Allowed fall in rate (difference between open and stop loss)	1.23773 – 1.23465 = 0.00308
Risk amount divided by the allowed fall in the exchange rate = position size	500 / 0.00308 = 162,337.66

Figure 2

So the calculated position size would be €162,337.00. Some brokers require position sizes to be in lots, or amounts that are made up of round one thousand figures. In such a case the above would be rounded down to 162k.

Except to define a limit, leverage should be irrelevant

Notice that the leverage allowed, in this case 100, does not figure in the calculation at all. The only consideration here is that the calculated position size should, when aggregated with any other trades that might be open, be less than what is allowed by the leverage, €5.00 MM. 162k is very comfortably below 5 million (it represents leverage usage of 3.24%).

Stop loss orders are very important. There are a number of inviolable rules attached to them. The first of these is that they are always, but always, used. Placing an order without a stop loss is an act of lunacy. The second rule is that they are only moved in the direction that will either reduce potential loss or increase profit.

The Omicron Forex software strategy carries out the above calculation automatically without the need for any inputs in the way of exchange rate (which is available to it instantaneously), stop loss level (which it calculates by reference to the trading plan that it incorporates), or equity size (money or money equivalents in the brokerage account), which is data it can obtain itself from the client account when the calculation needs to be made.

When placed, the trade would look like this on the 30 minute EUR/USD chart (the label "Entry level" has been added manually):

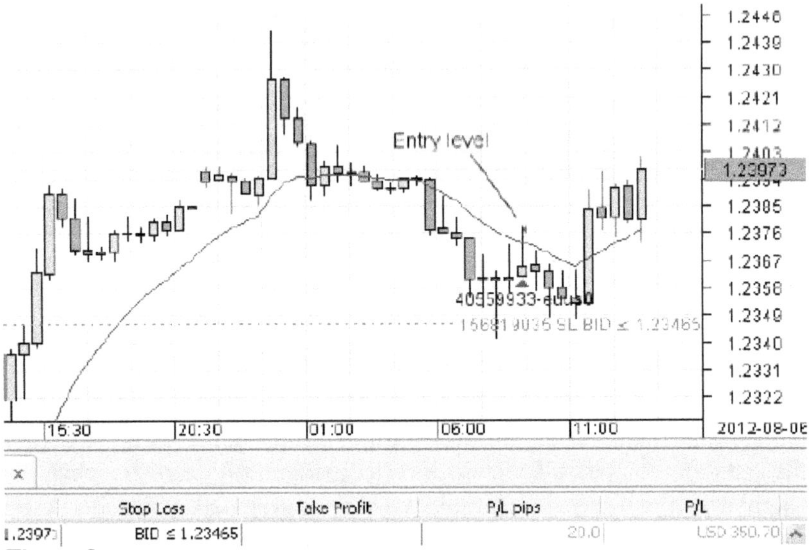

Figure 3

Diversification

There are those in the academic world who claim that diversification is a myth. The reason for this is that they have come to the conclusion that all asset classes in our global economy are correlated (move in harmony with each other). Traditional diversification involved investing in things that could be expected to do well when the others were doing badly. Think of a shop stocking umbrellas to favour winter revenues and something like barbecues to drive income in summer.

The diversification under discussion here is very much on the micro level. Individual currency traders might also decide to get involved in equities, for example, as a form of diversification, or may have property holdings for the same reason. That type of activity is beyond the scope of this manual. Here multiple currency pairs are used in an attempt to improve the risk profile that would be present if trading was confined to one currency pair only.

Even in Forex the proponents of what they call the myth of diversification are correct in the sense that anything that tends to cause short-term volatility for one currency will send ripples through many if not all currency pairs. It is not immediately obvious what effect the Bank of England Monetary Policy Committee meeting minutes should have on the AUD/USD pair, but they can cause a wave in both directions on that pair when they are released.

The Euro tends to march in lockstep with the British pound when all other things are equal for the two of them, and the Euro is also well correlated with the AUD, as both are classified as "risk-on" currencies. The USD is the ultimate "risk-off", or safe haven unit. Anything that is perceived to be bad for the global economy will strengthen the dollar no matter how dire the economic and / or monetary conditions in the USA might appear to be.

Our diversification can be expected to work because the currency pairs used, while they might be correlated, are not perfectly so. See the section on psychology for examples.

Do not confuse past and present

Another potential problem with diversification, but only for those traders whose mindset allows them to confuse the past with the present, is that sometimes when there are a number of positions on and one of them is going nowhere, regrets tend to surface for having placed the non-performing trade. They forget two things: one, that they are looking at the situation with the benefit of hindsight and two, that anything can happen in the future - the turkey they think they are looking at now could easily become a beautiful swan in a short time. Of course it could also become even worse, suffer a decline and go into reverse, but that is what our stop loss order is there for.

In practice, basically because of the possibility that losses will be incurred on one pair while another is making profits, the net outcome over time will not be that much different than if there was no diversification. The real benefit is that it tends to smooth things in the interim. Drawdowns (losses incurred on a daily, weekly or monthly basis) will be less severe at any given time than they otherwise might be, while periodic interim surpluses that might otherwise be present will be smaller. This is good for the psychology of trading, because there are few things more debilitating than facing large drawdowns, at the time they are experienced. It takes a lot of faith and sangfroid not to be affected by these for the simple reason that no matter what your system has tested like in the past, the future is, as always, an unknown country.

And here is where risk management and capital retention come together with a bang: when you diversify into one or more additional currency pairs, you must make sure to reduce position size for each one. You might decide that the benefits of diversification are such that the reduction does not need to be pro-rata. For example, if you include five pairs, you might only reduce your risk amount so that each pair had a quarter of what you would be prepared to risk where there was no diversification, meaning that your overall aggregated risk will be larger than if your entire stake was in one pair.

Chapter Six: Thinking in probabilities

In the market environment, reasons are irrelevant.

Mark Douglas: The Disciplined Trader

Probability theory was developed by early mathematicians as a means of assisting their aristocratic clients to prosper at the gaming tables. It was very quickly realised that the host, the person who controlled the roulette wheel or the blackjack bank, could build an advantage for themselves into the rules of the game. In roulette this now comes from the fact that all wheels contain a spot, labelled 0 and / or coloured yellow, where only the house can win. With a properly balanced wheel the odds in favour of any number winning are exactly equal but if there is one position on which only the house can win then, over a large number of plays, the house will always come out ahead.

Critical to success is the fact that the house, or in modern times the casino, looks on the whole matter over a period of a number of games, and not just on one, two turns of the wheel, or even an evening's gambling, which will be the time perspective of most players. In Europe there is only one zero on a roulette wheel. In the US there are two, making US roulette distinctly more disadvantageous to the player.

In Blackjack (or Vingt et Une, or Pontoon), the advantage for the banker comes from the fact that if a player goes bust (reaches a position where his cards add up to more than 21), the house wins, regardless of whether or not the banker goes bust at the end of that particular game. Some blackjack players are able to create an advantage for themselves by "counting cards", that is, noting the number and values of the cards that are upturned on the table in front of all players, including themselves, and adjusting their betting in accordance with what they then know to remain in the deck. This process is greatly resisted by casinos, and anyone found to be indulging in it will be barred and / or made subject to other punitive measures.

The lesson is clear when applied to trading. As the future cannot be foretold, in order to consistently make profits traders must have an edge which, in the nature of things, can only come when the activity is viewed on a long term perspective and over a number of trades. In equity trading, the market specialist (on the NYSE) or market maker (on the NASDAQ) holds inventory of stock and normally takes the other side of trades that are made by private participants through their brokers. In addition to that, the broker often holds stock as well and can also be the counterparty. This gives all these entities an opportunity to define an edge for themselves, which has to be, by definition, at the expense of the trader.

Far more preferable, from the point of view of the private trader, is to do business with what is known as an Electronic Communications Network (ECN) broker. Here all trades should be made directly between the party that wishes to buy and the one that wants to sell. All the broker does is facilitates the trade. His profits come from commissions, the spread (the small difference between the buy and sell price) and any charges that are applied to leveraged positions that are kept open overnight. Such brokers advertise themselves as having "no dealing desk". If the trades description acts in various jurisdictions have any meaning, this should turn out to be the case in practice.

Positive expectation

If the specialist, market maker and broker are all taken out of the equation and trades can be made directly between the buyers and sellers, then the way is at least open for individual traders to define an edge for themselves. Key to this is a positive expectation. This can come about in a combination of two ways: ensure that each winning trade is more profitable than the loss on any losing trade, and win more trades than are lost.

The trading plan programmed into the Omicron Forex trading software puts this into action by ensuring that the loss on any trade can be no more than between 0.8 % and 1% of equity while putting various measures in place to attempt to make wins much larger than that. The first thing that happens in any winning trade is that one half of the position is taken off when the profit reaches one percent of equity, while at the same time the stop loss order is moved towards the break even position, the exchange rate at which the trade was entered. Even at this stage profit has been locked in (minimum 0.5% if the trade now goes against the position) while leaving the door open to achieve theoretically uncapped profits on what has become a free trade in an amount that is equal to half the original position.

Fundamental to this is the ability to trust the broker to act on the provisional order that has been placed to achieve the outcome described. This is not always the case – brokers and their systems have been known to fall down in this area. This is why it is necessary to choose one that you can have confidence in.

This procedure has an importance that is on the same level as always using a stop loss. Think in probabilities - any given trade is not significant, and the future cannot be foretold. Therefore unrealised (or paper) profits attain a greater importance than they otherwise might appear to have. What this means in practice is they must be protected. Taking off some proportion of a trade, and moving to break-even at the earliest time, therefore becomes something that should, in principle, be done. Apart from that, the trader's back analysis of historical price action tells them that it is the right thing to do.

The objective

Many traders, even the most experienced, have a preconception that paper profits are in some manner inferior to profits that have been realised after the close of the trade. The successful trader does not allow this to be the case. To believe that part of your equity, which is what a paper profit constitutes, can be gambled with because it was not there earlier in the day when trading started is a major psychological mistake to make.

Just as paper profits must be protected like newborn babes, so losses must be ruthlessly and clinically cut down before they have a chance to develop.

The following is an example of the kind of trading combination you should aim for. Your systems should be designed so that you have a reasonable expectation of something like it happening on a regular basis, although there is certainly no guarantee that this will be the case. The following is not even an indication of a typical week. It has been chosen to illustrate the fundamental importance of having a mentality that fiercely protects 'paper' profits and ruthlessly cuts losses. The occasional profit foregone because the trailing stop algorithm has stopped out the trade too early, which becomes apparent in hindsight, is nothing more or less than the cost of doing business. All it means in reality is that you must be constantly testing, testing, testing and, very importantly, doing this over extended periods.

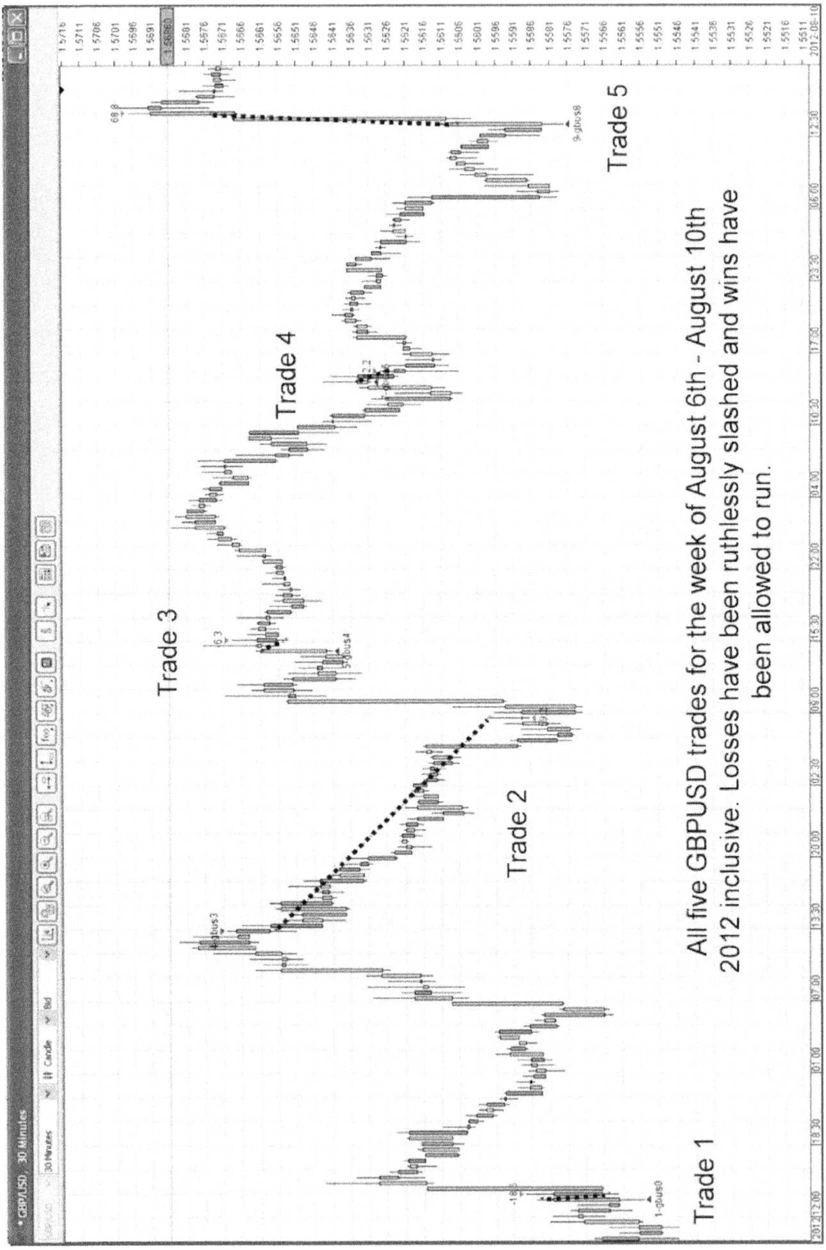
GBP/USD, 30 Minutes
Trade 1
Trade 2
Trade 3
Trade 4
Trade 5
All five GBPUSD trades for the week of August 6th - August 10th 2012 inclusive. Losses have been ruthlessly slashed and wins have been allowed to run.

During the course of the week starting on Monday August 6th 2012 and ending on Friday August 10th 2012 the Omicron Forex breakout algorithm made five trades. It could have made more but it is programmed to refrain from new trades when there are currently open positions under management. The example here deals with only one pair but in practice five pairs would be involved in trades simultaneously in order to get the benefits that accrue from diversification.

No day in that week was judged to be unsuitable for trading. In other words, no day was known in advance to be a day when there was a probability of bi-directional volatility of a type that would trigger the trades and their stops in rapid succession.

Trade number one was triggered and within the next hour the preset provisional stop loss order was also activated. Even though the overall short term trend favoured the trade, a very short term reversal was enough to close it out. The loss was in the order of 1% of equity.

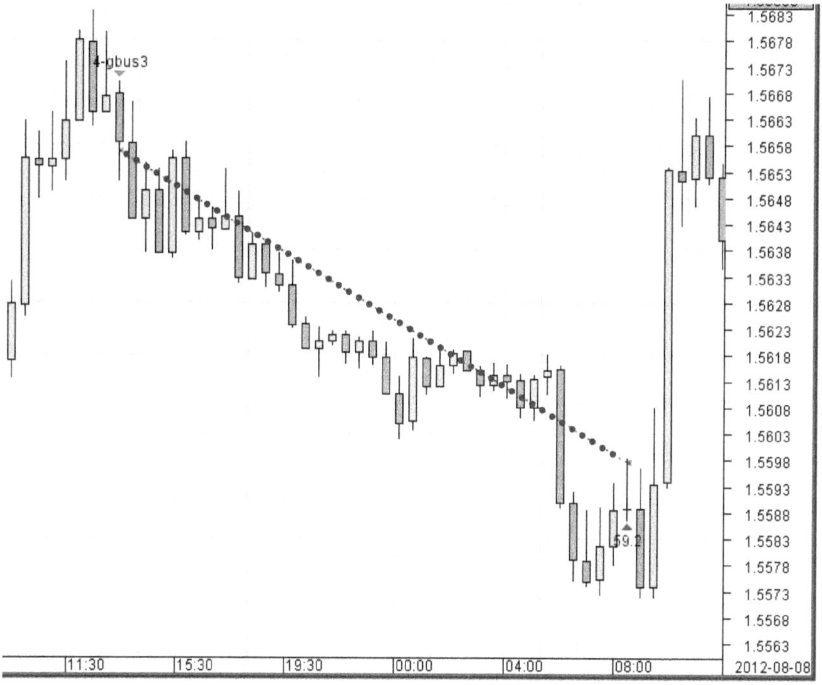

Trade number two was in the opposite direction to trade number one. It lasted for 20 hours. When the price action reversed into the trailing stop the overall gross profit booked was over 3% of equity.

Trades three and four: the next two trades were losses but, very significantly, these losses were minimised by the action of the trailing stop which started to move in the direction of cutting loss or increasing profit at an early stage after the trades were entered. The losses were 0.36% and 0.7% respectively.

Trade number five was also a significant winner, grossing nearly 4%. This trade would have been terminated at the close of London trading on the Friday in accordance with the policy of not holding trades over the weekend.

It might also be worth reiterating at this point that there is total indifference as to the direction of each trade. One of the wins was a SHORT trade and the other was LONG. There were more losses than wins, but the week still came out well ahead in terms of percentage profit. This is because there is a positive expectation at all times.

The net result for the week in Profit and Loss terms is below:

Closed orders:

Label	Amount	Direction	Open price	Close price	Profit/ Loss	P/L in pips	Open date and time	Close date and time
gbus0	0.27815	BUY	1.558	1.557	-517.36	-18.6	06/08/2012 13:44:27	06/08/2012 14:26:08
gbus3	0.27705	SELL	1.566	1.56	1632.66	58.9	07/08/2012 13:36:35	08/08/2012 08:42:25
gbus4	0.28555	BUY	1.566	1.565	-179.9	-6.3	08/08/2012 14:57:57	09/08/2012 15:50:08
gbus6	0.28405	BUY	1.563	1.562	-346.54	-12.2	09/08/2012 14:30:42	09/08/2012 15:33:10
gbus8	0.28145	BUY	1.561	1.568	1939.38	68.8	10/08/2012 13:49:19	10/08/2012 14:51:54
					2528.24			
				Commissions	82.14			
					2446.10			
					4.89%			

An outcome that represented a profit of 4.89% of equity net of commissions in a week would be an exceptional one. Many professional traders would be delighted to make this amount monthly, particularly if they could do so consistently.

Back-testing

Making sure that more trades are won than lost is somewhat more difficult but this is where price action research comes in. The automated strategies, under the control of the same software that places the trades, are applied to price data going back over time, often for many years. Data broken down into periods of one minute is available for these blocks of time. It is the later data that is most important because it is this activity that will best approximate to what is likely to happen in the immediate future.

There are various things that must be taken into account when this research, known as back-testing, is being carried out. One is to ensure that different time zones and periods of the year are taken into account. Even though the data used is always recorded by reference to Greenwich Mean Time (GMT), the various trading centres of the world operate in different time zones. New York is normally five hours behind London, but even that city, of which Greenwich is a suburb, operates on GMT + 1 hour when adjustment is made for daylight saving time in the summer. When using 30 minute charts, as the Omicron Forex breakout strategy does, such things can have high significance.

Traders need to do their own research and their own back-testing. While manuals like this can show what is possible and how it can be carried out, there is no substitute for achieving the work-rate yourself. You need to be able to see prices changing in the historical tester. You need to be able to change the strategy parameters, one by one, and note the effect it has on the outcome over a significant period of time, much more than a few days or a month. You must train yourself to recognise and avoid the phenomenon of curve-fitting, which means allowing yourself to be convinced that changes made that are effective in the short term can be extrapolated to the longer term. They cannot.

The historical tester allows for back-testing to be done in visual mode, when activity is so speeded up that 30 minute bars can open and close in seconds. As well as providing the answers to research questions this makes available a tremendously vivid representation of the behaviour of prices and highlights, in particular, the need to maintain the discipline required to allow each trade to take its course as part of an overall strategic plan which is based on probabilities.

Chapter Seven: Discipline, and an apparent contradiction

The test of a first-rate intelligence is the ability to hold two opposed ideas in the mind at the same time, and still retain the ability to function.

F. Scott Fitzgerald: "The Crack-Up" (1936)

A fundamentally important requirement for trading, whether it is Forex or anything else, is the ability to maintain discipline. This sounds great, but what does it mean in practice?

It means having a plan and sticking to it. It means realising that, in the context of a well tested strategy, any one trade is verging on the insignificant. Knowing this, no trader would intervene, for example, to move his or her stop out of sequence to that specified in the plan. They most certainly would not make policy on the fly and do something like increasing the stop loss distance after the trade had been placed, for any reason.

Trading in a methodical manner in accordance with the plan, and having the discipline to do it continuously, is known as systematic trading. The opposite of this is discretionary trading. Here a trader will watch for opportunities and act on them. The trigger for entering a position might be a news story, a remark by a commentator or nothing more sophisticated than gut feeling. This type of trading is not recommended (some market commentators seem to be there as contrarian indicators - one would make more profit by doing precisely the opposite of what they recommend), but it can be very difficult at times to stay on the train tracks that are mandated by systematic trading.

Automated routines are one way of helping to overcome this difficulty. At the very least, if you find yourself intervening in the operation of one of them you will know that discipline has been breached. This is an advance over making an intervention and being under the illusion that it was part of the strategy just because you considered at one stage making such a change in the plan but decided, for now, not to. A proper plan is not, repeat not, modified in the heat of the moment.

Discretion required

Having said all that, there are times when discretion is required. This might sound like a contradiction but there is nothing illogical about making an element of discretion part of the plan. After all, it has been recognised that, helpful as automation is in trading, the idea of a true Forex robot, set to run once and never to be monitored or managed, is the proverbial non-runner – a recipe for account disaster. And, given the unbounded nature of the complexity of trading, is likely to remain so.

One occasion where discretion is called for is on those special announcement days that so effect the Forex market. In the example below, a scheduled announcement has been made by the US Federal Open Market Committee (FOMC), basically to the effect that they were leaving interest rates unchanged, at 16:30 GMT, or 12:30 in New York, on June 20th 2012. These announcements take place on what has become known as Fed Day, which occurs about 11 times per year, and is always scheduled well in advance. "No change" on this occasion did not prevent large spikes in opposite directions in the EUR/USD pair immediately after the announcement. These would have blown any new trade taken at the opening of London or NY out of the water.

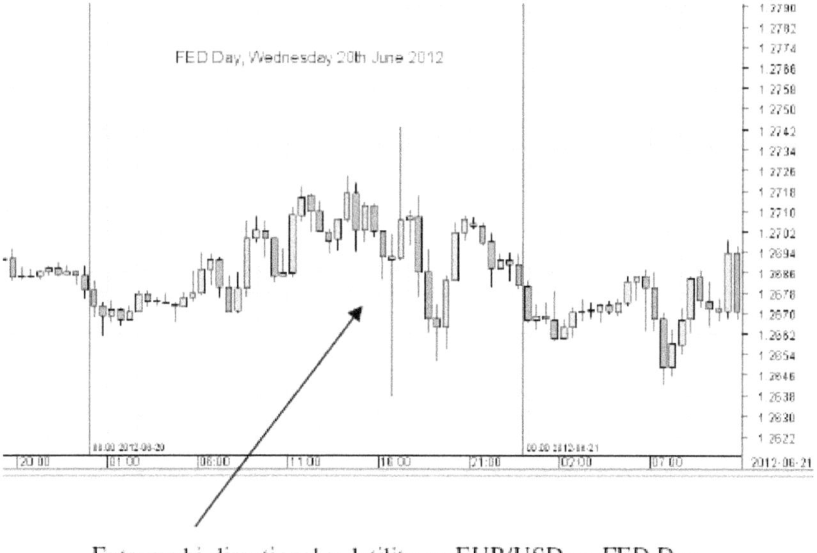

Extreme bi-directional volatility on EUR/USD on FED Day

It was known that the announcement was coming up, and when, and also the tendency of the market to behave in the way it did on such occasions. There is no point at all in knowingly sending your troops (your equity funds) into a hail of bullets. Therefore, we have to find another way of dealing with such events. Experience has shown that certain announcements, for example US quarterly GDP figures, can be accommodated by waiting until some hours after the announcement before setting up a trade.

Working out the characteristics of the way the market is likely to behave for different scheduled events, and the way the patterns change over time, is where the real work is involved in currency trading. Spend a lot of time doing just that - in Forex, this is where having a good work rate is important. Apart from events that can affect EUR/USD, there are those that are likely to be more critical to the movement of other currency pairs when they take place in the countries that use them. Examples are interest rate decisions and commentary by the Bank of England or the Reserve Bank of Australia (RBA) where pairs involving the GBP and / or the AUD are concerned.

For some scheduled announcements a very valid option is to simply make a strategic withdrawal on that day, and sit on the sidelines.

Of course there are also times when it is impossible to anticipate developments. Below is an example of a trade that started off well on the release of German business confidence data, which was deemed a positive for the Euro. Note well that it was not necessary to have been aware of this beforehand. The system is designed to latch on to movements such as this when they occur, for whatever reason.

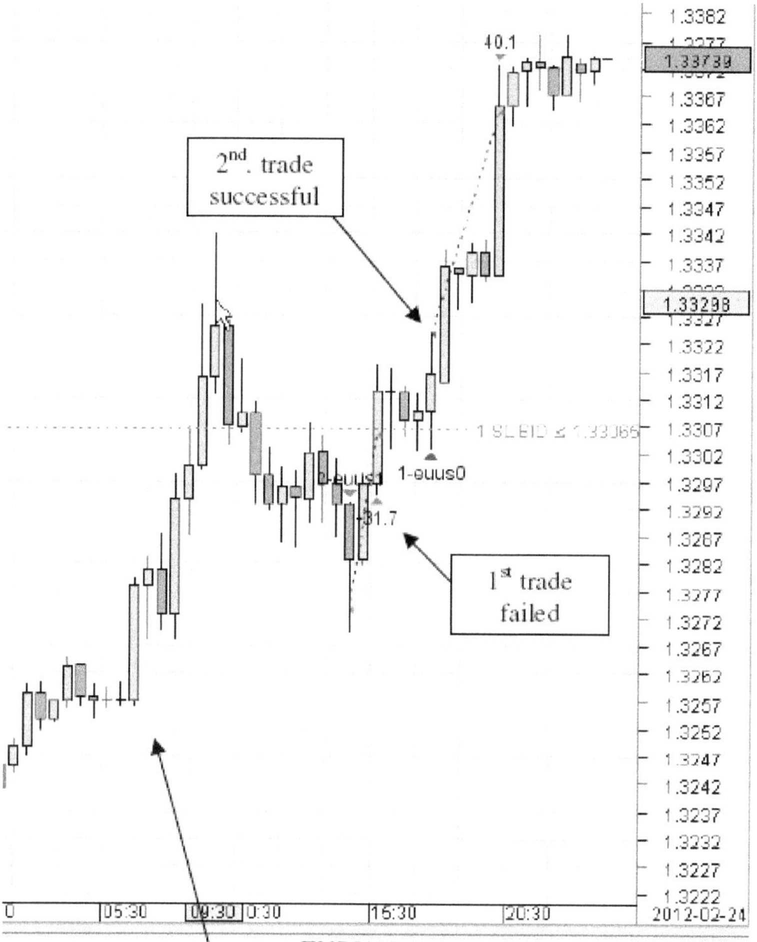

EURUSD 30 minutes

The Euro started to rise against the US dollar. So far, so good. Then, at about 9:30 GMT the EU Commission came out with an announcement that it expected the euro zone (the bloc made up of those countries that use the euro as currency) to go back into recession. This was perceived, for a short time, as negative for the euro. The system had set itself up on that day on the 13:00 GMT bar and the downward swing caused a short order to be triggered. This was stopped out for a loss when the market had second thoughts about the EU Commission announcement and continued its original rise based on the earlier good news. The Omicron Forex breakout strategy caught this new rise as well, for a profit, but the roller coaster ride of that day did do a small amount of damage because the default stop was hit on the original short trade.

WORLD FOREX: Euro Rallies On Strong German Business Confidence

-- Euro trades at strongest level against dollar since Dec. 12

-- Strong German Ifo survey buoys optimism

-- ...but rally fizzles out ahead of $1.3350 as EC forecasts euro-area recession

...

By Jessica Mead
Of DOW JONES NEWSWIRES

LONDON -(Dow Jones)- The euro rose in European hours Thursday to its highest level against the dollar since early December as strong German business confidence data helped to buoy investor confidence in the wobbly global economy, even as crude oil prices hit new nine-month highs.

...

However, tempering this optimism was news the European Commission now expects the euro zone to slip back into recession this year with an economic contraction of 0.3% in real gross domestic product in the first quarter, after a similar decline in the last three months of 2011.

...

-By Jessica Mead, Dow Jones Newswires; +44 (0) 20 7842 9256, jessica.mead@dowjones.com; @djfxtrader/@jessicacmead

(Dow Jones Technical Strategist Francis Bray in London, Niclas Rolander in Stockholm and Kjetil Malkenes Hovland in Oslo contributed to this story.)

(END) Dow Jones Newswires

February 23, 2012 07:17 ET (12:17 GMT)

Dow Jones Newswire report explaining one reversal, but not two.

Other considerations: support and resistance

It is tempting to second guess the system and, for example, to change the way the software sets up the conditional orders after they have been placed but before they are actually filled. This might happen when you notice that major support or resistance levels are coming into view. However, this is to second guess matters. Attempting to predict market direction is nearly always a mistake. For this reason you should confine yourself to using discretion only in order to decide when to sit out a trading day, or to make the trigger bar of the system one that comes into being on a high impact announcement day a number of hours after the event that has the potential to increase short term bi-directional volatility. The decision on whether or not to do this will be based on research into how the price acted on previous, similar, occasions.

Two types of volatility

Volatility is the measure of the rate at which prices or exchange rates change. This has little to do with the volume of business – volatility can be quite high during times of thin trading, because relatively small traders have the ability to move the market on those occasions. For the purposes of the Omicron Forex breakout strategy, distinction is made between two types of volatility. The bi-directional kind, which can hit the stops in rapid succession, is a major issue for all breakout trade methods and efforts are put into avoiding the markets when it is high. Uni-directional volatility, where the price takes off in one or other direction and just keeps on going, is a different matter. This kind is loved by breakout traders and they often experience feelings of dismay when it is found that they are not in the market when it happens.

Chapter Eight: Psychology

To be, or not to be: that is the question:
Whether 'tis nobler in the mind to suffer
The slings and arrows of outrageous fortune,
Or to take arms against a sea of troubles,
And by opposing end them?

William Shakespeare: Hamlet

The psychology of trading is yet another concept that a lot is heard about but which all too often remains just that, a concept. The best way, and some would argue the only way, to gain an understanding of what it really means is to indulge in a great deal of screen time – time spent trading with either a live account or a demo account where you never reset the account values. Or using an automated strategy on historical data with visual output. What can be done here is to explain what you would be expected to find out under such conditions.

The purpose of trading, contrary to what new entrants to the activity might think, is not to make money. Far more important than this for the human psyche is the need to be proved correct – it just happens that very often the accumulation of profits defines and measures what success looks like. Psychology is all about perceptions. Each person's idea of what the world is like is different because nobody has a perfect view of reality. What each has is a mental image that is the result of the interpretation of the signals received by the senses, as related to and interacting with experiences that have been acquired during life, particularly those from early on. Therefore, if you can convince yourself that being correct in your trading activity is not about making money, at least from the very start, and instead is about training yourself to work within parameters that define success *whether or not* you are profitable, you will be better able to proceed.

Essential tools for peace of mind

Tools that enable you to achieve this include a trading plan, a strategy that is based on the probability of being right in aggregate over a period of time rather than in any given trade, and a gradual, methodical approach to the amounts that you invest in your trading.

The first thing to do is to define and live the parameters for your trading. For example, if you decide that the total amount you will risk on any trade is 2% of equity and the trade goes against you, success in this case is defined by ensuring that your loss is, in fact, no more than that amount. The trade went the wrong way – so what? You made sure that you capped your loss at 2% when the trade closed, therefore living up to your principle. What you have is a successful application of one part of your strategy. So long as the same can be said for all other parts, this is all that matters because you are in for the long haul, you are conscious that the results over many trades are what count and you are *thinking in probabilities*.

Of course, it is important that you have confidence in the other strategy elements as well. But you know that the next trade you take will be mandated according to research that has proven that such methodology worked in the past. The standard financial products disclaimer that says that past performance is not a guarantee of future performance is certainly valid, but your trading is a tiny part of a market that has shown patterns continuously and, in the event that the market turns completely on its head, you have strong and effective money management techniques in place. Of particular assistance is the knowledge that, no matter what, in each successful trade a percentage of the profit will be taken off when the level of gain reaches a set point, currently 1% for our strategy, and the stop loss will be moved towards break-even, making the rest of the trade costless or nearly so in terms of risk. Yet more comfort can be provided by a level of diversification.

Diversification in Forex

Many currency pairs are correlated – in other words, their historical charts for any given period look similar, but, apart from special cases that arise from time to time, this correlation is far from perfect. To best illustrate this it might be instructive to look at one of the special cases, where the correlation is as close to perfect as you can get, although negatively so. The two pairs are the EUR/USD and the USD/CHF (CHF is the symbol for the Swiss franc), and the correlation comes about as a direct result of the decision by the Swiss monetary authorities to intervene in the market to ensure that the franc does not fall to below the level of 1.20 to the Euro. This was done because money was flooding into Swiss francs as a response to the perception that the Euro was in crisis and the consequent appreciation of the franc was hurting exports of Swiss manufactured goods. The Swiss franc (CHF) had become a “safe haven” currency (“CH” stands for “Confoederatio Helvetica”, which is the Latin version of “Swiss Confederation”, the official name of Switzerland).

First, the daily graph of EUR/CHF over the first months of 2012:

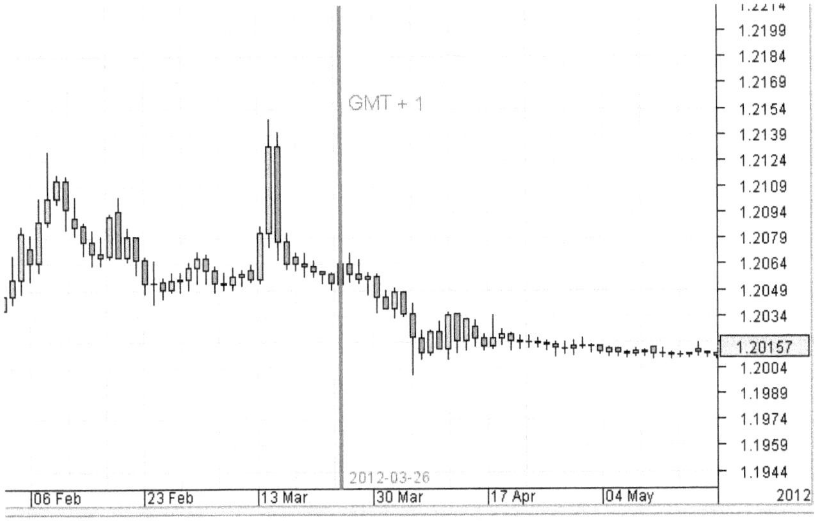

Figure 4: Daily chart of EURCHF

This clearly shows the convergence to the 1.20 area. The natural tendency is for the Swiss franc to continue to appreciate (for EUR/CHF pair to go down), but as it does so, the Swiss National Bank (SNB) intervenes in the market to keep it close to 1.20 against the Euro.

Now look at EUR/CHF as compared to USD/CHF:

Figure 5

They are mirror images of each other, for all intents and purposes. This is because, while EUR/CHF has been fixed, the US dollar continues to change relative to the Euro. The pairs are said to be negatively correlated (Remember, however, that this has not the same significance as if two equities were negatively correlated - the order of the currency pairs has been arbitrarily fixed by convention).

And at EUR/USD as compared to EUR/AUD (AUD is the Australian dollar):

Figure 6

You can see that although the basic direction at any given time might be roughly the same, there are substantial divergences. These two pairs have been more closely correlated in the past, but never perfectly. The same goes for many others and it is the small differences that provide protection in the way of diversification. Our strategy calls for positions to be taken on five pairs at present. Because of continuous research on the way they behave, this could change. Right now the five pairs are:

EUR/USD
EUR/GBP
EUR/AUD
USD/GBP
USD/CAD

Do not lose sight of the fact that position sizes must be reduced pro-rata for any additional currency pairs you decide to trade in order to make sure that the aggregate amount put at risk does not exceed the percentage of equity allowed at a given time.

Build up gradually as you gain confidence

Yet another element for providing peace of mind is the gradual build up of the amounts that are committed to trading. You should start with a demo account, where you will risk no money at all, although any profits you make will also be of the imaginary kind. As you gain confidence with your real-money account you can start to use a greater sum as your base equity, which are the funds upon which all percentages mentioned in these notes are based. Then, as time goes by and you get more and more in tune with what you are doing you can add to your account until you reach the amount that you wish, and can afford, to trade with.

Chapter Nine: Fundamental and technical analysis

The game taught me the game. And it didn't spare me rod while teaching.

Jesse Livermore: Reminiscences of a Stock Operator

Technical analysis is concerned with taking trades based on the way currencies are expected to perform when certain chart based technical signals are present. Fundamental analysis is about the way the markets react to financial, political and other such developments that take place.

When it comes to events in the outside world that might move the markets, there are two basic categories to be taken into account – scheduled and unscheduled. However, our only interest in scheduled events is for the likelihood of them resulting in bi-directional volatility. It is normally not possible to know what announcements will contain and, even after they are known, what effects they will have on the eventual direction of the markets.

And it is this last consideration that is important. There is no scarcity of pundits who are willing to attempt to predict things, and to attempt to anticipate what a currency pair will do if they are right. The reality is that they have, by this practice, simply magnified the chances of being wrong. They might get the prediction right, but be wrong about the market reaction. On the other hand the prediction might be wrong, in which case they lose credibility. It is far better to concentrate on what the market is actually doing in the aftermath of any development. This requires the study of present tense price action, which we trade with just one eye to how market participants have reacted in the past to the fundamentals. They can certainly surprise you. On the other hand, expectations of these reactions by others can become a self-fulfilling prophecy.

Past, present and future

There are many technical indicators and techniques based on the way they form themselves for picking market direction, most of which have come from the technical analysts that study and trade the equity markets. Technical indicators include Stochastics, MACD, Bollinger Bands, Floor Trader Pivots, Ichimoko Clouds and many, many more. Each and every one of them suffers from one drawback – they are all lagging indicators. This means that they form and reform based on what has already happened, not on what is happening now.

There are only three tenses – past, present and future. Studying the future is ruled out because, no matter what, nobody is clairvoyant - it is impossible to foretell what will happen. That leaves the past and the present. The past is gone and will never return. Even though patterns, of a sort, appear and reappear on charts of prices and exchange rates against time, they are never identical.

The present at least tells what is happening now. What is happening now, of course, can stop happening and reverse, but activity in the present rather than the past has a better chance of signifying the way forward, and if things do turn around, risk management systems are in place, and are well tried and tested.

Chart patterns, and support and resistance

Apart from the lagging technical indicators there are recognised chart patterns, such as head and shoulders formations, double and triple tops and bottoms, flags and pennants, that do seem to command respect, probably because so many traders believe in them. Support and resistance levels, which are signified by repeated failed attempts to breach them, also work, at least temporarily. What always surprises is the degree to which these form at round numbers on the chart. By any standards, a round number should not have any particular significance, just as the millennium year of 2000 had no significance in terms of natural phenomena, and in any event was celebrated at the wrong time due to ignorance of the importance of zero on the number line. These things are relevant only because of the way the human mind works but that, of course, is a valid consideration in trading because all other traders are human, or at least have had their software written by humans.

That support and resistance levels are respected is only important if they actually result in a change in the trend. A support line that is eventually breached is one that the trader will be happy he or she did not react to. There are scalpers who operate in the very short term, and who watch for these and act on them, but this is high octane stuff.

Other chart patterns are those made up of the relative positions of open, close, top and bottom of candlestick bars. These have various names, such as exhaustion bars (or pin bars), where the open and close are near the top or bottom of a long bar, inside bars which, as the name suggests, are formed within the top and bottom of the one that preceded them, and the Hikkake pattern, which is a combination of inside bar and a false move outside of the so called mother bar, or the one before, and which helps define, the inside bar. These patterns are said to have predictive powers about either a reversal or a continuation of a trend. These are in direct contradiction and the problem is you cannot really tell which of them it is until after the fact, when it is often too late to take advantage.

Key dates in the trading calendar

Fundamental analysis of currency markets takes in such things as the political, fiscal, monetary and commercial health of the economy whose currency might be considered as one side of a trade. While these things certainly change and influence exchange rates in the long term, all market participants are now carefully watching what are considered to be leading indicators. The market can react very quickly indeed to an announcement that might have a bearing on future trends.

So it is important to be aware of the times at which important announcements will be made. Some of these are on fixed days every month, such as the U.S. non-farm payroll report which is released at 08:30 EST on the first Friday of the month, to cover the previous month, by the US Department of Labor. The day before, a private company, ADP Payroll Services Inc., a Human Resources outsource concern, publishes research from an analysis of its own records that is widely perceived to be an early warning of what the NFP figures will contain.

Both of these are watched carefully, and are perhaps the announcements which, at the time of writing, can be expected to have the biggest effect on currency pairs that include the US dollar, although there are others that can sometimes have a greater impact. The market reaction is nearly always a dramatic increase in bi-directional volatility at the time of the announcement, often with strong uni-directional moves or even new trends developing in the hours and days that follow.

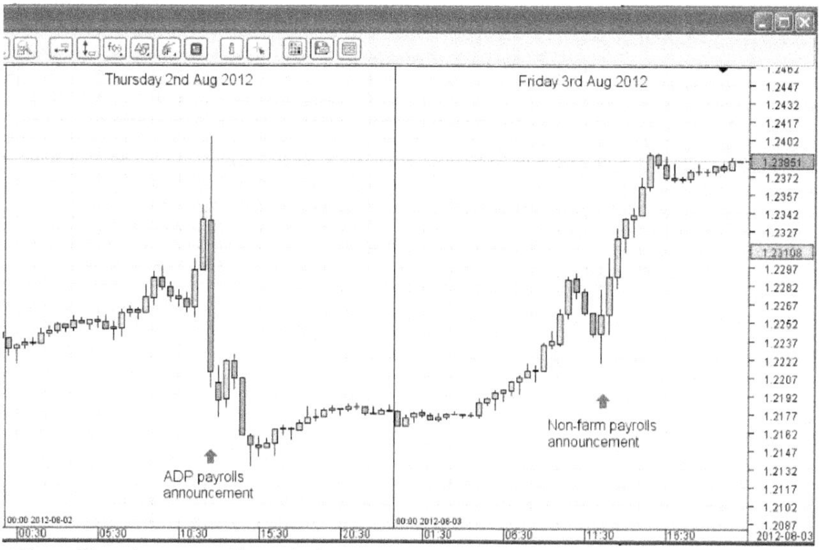

The effect that payroll statistics announcements can have on the EUR/USD

Below is a list of some of the more important announcement types for the Forex market. This list is not exhaustive, nor is the importance of each announcement fixed. Sometimes an event in this list will cause hardly a ripple, while at other times one or other will be awaited with bated breath by participants. This normally coincides with times of crisis, or perceived crisis, in an economy. For example, during the Euro crisis that started in 2008, sovereign bond auctions, which are normally regarded as routine events, came to be carefully watched for the interest rate that had to be paid and the take-up of the offering, if the Euro zone member state involved was perceived to be a potential bailout candidate.

Potential high impact events for Forex
Consumer confidence indices, esp. Michigan Consumer Sentiment Index in the USA
Interest rate announcements, particularly from the FOMC, ECB, Bank of England, Reserve Bank of Australia (RBA) and the Bank of Canada
News conferences by central banks, and testimony to lawmakers by central bank heads
Payrolls, including US non-farm payrolls and ADP report
Jobless claims
Inflation rate announcements, (PPI = Producer Price Inflation, CPI = Consumer Price Index)
GDP growth or contraction announcements
Commentary on current economic conditions (Beige book in the USA)
Purchasing Managers Index (PMI) (Non government indicator)
House price indices (Non government indicator)
Durable goods reports, especially in the USA
Business inventories
Bond auctions in various jurisdictions

Potential high impact events for Forex trading

In addition to the above there can be totally unscheduled commentary from influential people like, for example, leading members of one or other of the central banks. These are, by their nature, impossible to predict. Again, a person perceived to be influential can say something on one occasion that is ignored, while at other times what might appear to the private trader as an innocuous comment from the same individual can move the market.

Watch the economic calendar carefully so that an assessment can be made of any likely impact of these and other announcements, in conjunction with the current economic and financial conditions. The most heavily traded currency pair is the EUR/USD, so developments in the US and Europe are likely to be significant. All the majors are interlinked, to a greater or lesser extent, but actions of the various central banks, for example, will obviously have a greater impact on their own currencies.

Interest rate differentials – the Carry Trade

Normally interest rate moves are an indication of the strength of an economy, and they impact Forex for this reason. Often, though, they are of supreme importance to those that participate in what is known as the Carry Trade.

When institutions change large amounts of their money into another currency they are interested in something other than the appreciation of that currency unit against the one they held previously. They are also motivated by what they can earn in interest by loaning the money. If one Central Bank has allowed the interest rate to rise in the jurisdiction it has responsibility for, for whatever reason, then institutions and hedge funds may try to target the yield they can get by borrowing a low interest currency, converting it into a high yielding one, loaning it out and pocketing the difference between the two rates. This is called the Carry Trade. A large differential in interest yield between two currencies will tend to cause an appreciation of the one with the higher interest yield because there will be a greater demand for this for carry trade purposes.

Very often traders take a view on whether or not the interest rate associated with a particular currency will rise in the future and bid up the currency in anticipation. As it rises, the interest rate is said to be getting “priced in”. This can happen almost imperceptivity over time when, for example, many traders take a view at the same time that a monetary authority will raise or reduce interest rates in the coming months.

Chapter Ten: Broker selection

The first thing brokers did after they organized the New York Stock Exchange was to stick the public with fixed commissions that lasted for the next 180 years.

Dr. Alexander Elder: Trading for a Living

Choosing the correct broker is of vital importance

Your choice of broker for your Forex trading is important. In deciding the features you would like him to have you can do little better than consider what the professional traders in the large institutions and hedge funds would regard as normal requirements. Fortunately, with the exception of commission rates (the pros get preferential treatment because of the large volumes they handle in their trades) practically all these things are now available to the private trader. But you need to know where to look. This will sometimes depend on the jurisdiction in which you do your trading.

Introducing agents programs

Most brokers have introducing agents' programs, where websites can get paid for introducing clients. The ones mentioned here are no exception. However, Omicron Forex's commitments to its clients and viewers are that (1) when a broker company is named it will have been ascertained that it fulfils all the requirements that have been identified here as being essential to give a service to private traders and (2) an exclusive introducing arrangement will never be entered into with any broker.

To be avoided

Brokers that take the other side of a trade are to be avoided. True ECN (stands for Electronic Communication Network in this case, which is not very explanatory) brokers are part of a network that receives bids and offers from large institutions and whose trading platform allows the private trader to deal directly with these institutions as the counterparty to the trade. The broker gets a reasonable commission for this service. He also pockets the spread, which is the difference between the ASK and the BID price of any currency pair.

Commissions, spreads and other costs

The commissions and spreads must themselves be reasonable. The spread should be the same for all traders but the commissions are normally related to the size of your trading account. ***Beware of brokers who advertise "no commissions" at all***. These will almost certainly have very wide spreads, which will result in you paying a lot more for each "round trip", or buy and sell transaction that you participate in. Always remember that it is the accumulated cost of many trades that is important. The cost of high spreads can be insidious - they can build up over time in a way that is not at all transparent.

In the book "Reminiscences of a stock operator" by Edwin Lefèvre, much mention is made of what were then known (in the 1920s) as "bucket shops", where anyone could take a position on the rise and fall of the stock of a quoted company. These outfits never dealt in the underlying share and seem to have had more in common with a casino or turf accountant that with a stock broker. They still exist, albeit in a slightly different form. They are characterised by phrases like "spread betting" and "CFD" trading, stock and Forex quotes that do not go beyond four decimal places and large spreads. If you are tempted to use one of these you should ask yourself if this is the type of intermediary a professional trader in a large institution would use. The answer is, of course, emphatically no.

Brokers that use the JForex trading platform, on which the Omicron Trading software strategies can be used:

Dukascopy Bank, Switzerland and European Union.
www.dukascopy.com

Alpari, USA, UK
www.alpari.com

FXDD, based in Malta, serving Europe and the USA.
www.fxdd.com

If you open an account with Dukascopy you will automatically be provided with the JForex trading platform. With the others you will have to specify you need this platform. The Metatrader platform is more widely available.

Chapter Eleven: The Forex trading plan: strategy defined

"In preparing for battle I have always found that plans are useless, but planning is indispensable."

Dwight D. Eisenhower

There is some potential for ambiguity here due to the fact that the good people at Dukascopy bank who developed the programming API of the JForex trading platform chose to call the finished Java software output "Strategies". (In the case of the MetaTrader platform, developed by MetaQuotes Software Corp., the software routines that do the same job are called "Expert Advisors", or EAs for short. Are these more examples of the old adage that programmers should never be allowed to have anything to do with naming conventions or text output in the programs they code?)

In any event, the type of strategy discussed in this section is in the original sense of the term, that of planning and directing operations, in this case successful Forex trading. Omicron Forex supplies the software strategies too, but the two must not be confused.

A holistic treatment

Planning must be holistic, that is to say it should take account of every aspect of the trading experience. There is no point, for example, in having a great method for choosing a trade if your Internet connection is likely to fail completely from time to time. Remember that even when a particular Forex function is automated you must monitor its progress at all times. This does not mean that you have to sit in front of the screen all day (such behaviour would be counterproductive, as boredom or something akin to it would eventually set in) but you must be in control and this means being able to check positions, the progress of trades and the initiation of new ones whenever you choose or feel you need to do so.

Implementing the strategy means understanding clearly that you operate a routine, each element of which can only be changed by using a formal, previously defined, change routine.

In proprietary trading, where individuals are employed by hedge funds, banks and other institutions to trade using the firm's money, there are a number of criteria that are applied in order to measure performance. These include calculating profit and loss, monitoring the equity curve (the gradual build up [or reduction] of account size related to time), the ratio of gains to losses, the largest winning and losing trades, average win and loss, the ratio of winning to losing trades and the average time in winning or losing trades.

There may also be limits placed on the maximum daily drawdown and position size. In Forex, it is normally required that all positions should be closed at the weekends. This is to guard against the development of "gaps" which can have the effect of making stop loss orders ineffective.

All of these elements should be part of the trading plan for a private trader too.

Targets for the most important limits

Profit & Loss: Not less than 4% profit per month averaged over the trailing three months. The equity curve should reflect this as the months go by.

Ratio of winning to losing trades: Consistently greater than 1 (which means that losing trades should not be more than 50% of all trades taken).

Largest winning and losing trades: Winning as large as possible, while losing trade amounts should be consistent with money management criteria.

Typical risk parameters:

Never risk more than 2% on any trade.

If losses reach 6% in any given month, trading should be suspended for the rest of that month.

Trading plan components

Change protocol

A true trading plan should be prepared by each trader individually. This is important in order to not miss out on what might be called the magic, or synergy, that comes from making it your own creation. Above all, it is important to understand the reasons why the plan is such a vital element: it is because, without it, the trader would wind up making decisions about important matters on the fly. Having given time to practicing and getting the required experience so that you can prepare the plan in the first instance, it is incumbent that the trader does not deviate from it, under any circumstances. If the plan calls for trading only certain currency pairs, which it should, it would be a violation to suddenly decide to trade a pair that was not in the plan. There is, of course, nothing to stop you changing the plan, but doing this must be a formal process involving research into the benefits and otherwise of making the change. This process should involve a time element – when you get the idea of adding a new pair (in this example) it should not be possible on principle to even implement the change before a period of some days has elapsed, and even then it must have been incorporated in the new and now current version of the plan.

So the very first part of the trading plan involves the protocol for making changes to it.

Mobilisation

Every project plan has a mobilisation phase and the one you are preparing for the deadly serious business of Forex trading is no exception. For these purposes, mobilisation is involved with deciding what you will need in the way of space, equipment and other physical requirements to allow you to operate comfortably and effectively, and then providing yourself with all of these things.

Space: You will need some kind of an area that is cut off from the rest of your dwelling, where you can set up your computer and operate without interruption. This could indeed be your bedroom or a spare room in the house. The important thing is that it is your domain and you will be able to operate without being disturbed.

Equipment: Undoubtedly the most important item under this heading is your computer and Internet connection. You will need a robust machine but there is no need to go overboard. The hardware requirements of Forex trading do not come anywhere near those of gaming, for example. The writer has a six year old Dell Dimension with a dual core processor, a sizeable hard disk, a CD Rom drive and 3.5 inch floppy drive, although he cannot remember the last time he used the floppy drive. It operates under Windows XP, Service Pack 3. This is starting to show its age now and an upgrade to Windows 7 must be contemplated, but it continues to work fine. Much more important for peace of mind is the backup that exists in the form of a Dell Inspiron laptop with a similar spec to the PC.

Internet connection is a 25 Mb. DSL connection. This is very high speed and before it came along trading took place comfortably on a 5Mb connection. As with the hardware, of more importance is the backup maintained. This is a mobile USB stick from a different service provider which can be switched over to in minutes if the main supply goes down for any reason. The USB Mobile broadband stick (modem) is designed for use in a laptop on the road but it works just fine with the PC as well. It has been needed about two or three times in the past year when the DSL supplier decided to carry out repairs or maintenance without bothering to give any notice.

When you use the JForex trading platform everything you need is downloaded each time you log on. Metatrader resides on the local PC but in operation is very similar to JForex – both systems transmit order instructions to the broker's server, where they are stored. What you will require on your computer is a version of **Java** that is greater than V5.0. V7.0 was made available recently and this should be used. It's available for free download from the Oracle Computer Company. You should familiarize yourself with the Java section of the Windows Control Panel. Very occasionally it will be necessary to clear the Java cache if you find you cannot connect to the JForex platform.

Instruments to be traded

The following represent a typical list of five pairs:

EUR/USD
EUR/GBP
EUR/AUD
USD/GBP
USD/CAD

This could change in the future and may even have changed by the time you read this. These pairs have been chosen now because back-testing indicates that they give an element of risk reduction through diversification. This feature does not necessarily improve long-term profitability but it does tend to smooth out the valleys and peaks that would otherwise exist in the equity curve. It is important, from the point of view of market psychology, to avoid the trauma of large draw downs.

Times to trade

Under the Omicron Forex automated strategies, getting into a trade is a two stage process. First, conditional trades, complete with stop loss orders (also conditional), are placed at either side of the breakout channel the software has calculated. It does this at the end of the time period bar on the chart that has been supplied to the routine as a user-defined parameter. Then, if and when the price goes to the level of one of these, the order is triggered and becomes an active order. It is necessary to make the time bar for placing the conditional order part of your trading plan. This might be different for each pair and will be determined from time to time by back-testing. At present the values of these bars have been determined for the various pairs but this could change. Any changes will only be activated by reference to the change parameter policy as previously mentioned.

Times not to trade

As stated before, there are days when no trades at all should be attempted. A good example is on the day before the US Non-Farm Payrolls report, when the ADP Company issues its assessment of the employment situation. Another is what has become known as FED Day, when the US Federal Reserve issues its interest rate decision and commentary. On these days volatility in both directions can be high, which creates false breakouts that adversely affect our strategy. The definite non-trading days should be listed in the plan and it should be made a part of the plan to study the Economic Calendar each week to define those other days, on a week-to-week basis, when traders should sit on the sidelines.

Risk parameters

These will be as enunciated at the start of this chapter but possibly modified in the light of your experience over time with the benefits or otherwise of the level of diversification that has been built into the plan.

Record keeping

It is important to be able to go back and study the trades that the system has made, and how they performed. This furthers your understanding of how price action works. This will almost certainly have a different feel depending on the currency pair involved. The trading platform you use will have good record keeping capability but it is up to you to access this every day and archive your records in a way that you can usefully retrieve in the future.

In the same way that keeping a ship's log is a fundamental part of the training and professional performance of a ship's captain, keeping a trade journal should be at the heart of every trader's activity. Short, relevant comments about the highlights of the day should be entered in it. It might be that the particular day in question was a Non-Farm Payrolls day, or it might have nothing to do with actual trading at all, just a note of something that affected the time you might have otherwise spent at the computer, such as having to attend a friend's wedding (traders are actually allowed to relax from time to time).

Being able to record screen shots of currency charts is immensely useful for the trade journal. Software that facilitates this, and which has been used for the chart illustrations in this manual, is called

Wisdom-soft ScreenHunter. At the time of writing the basic version is completely free. It is available for download at:

http://www.wisdom-soft.com/products/screenhunter.htm

The records must be used

Then these records you have collected must be made use of. This means going back over them on a regular basis, not less often than once a week, in order to learn from the experiences you have had. How did each trading pair react to the various GDP reports when they were announced, and in the days following? What effect, if any, did the European Central Bank (ECB) monthly announcement and press conference make on the day and later? Was there an unscheduled event that moved the markets, for example a downgrade of a country by one or more of the rating agencies? Did your broker's server go down (a serious event, but you know your system will be reliable because you have taken the precautions outlined above). It is important to bear in mind that it is the reaction of the currency markets to developments in the economy, politics or global affairs that are significant, not the events themselves. The reaction is, very often, counterintuitive.

Decide on a level of recording that you are happy with and describe it in the plan. Some people are comfortable with copious recording and if this is you, do it. Others find the minimum to be enough. What is vital is that you have sufficient records to be able to go back and analyse each trade that took place. This is of particular importance in the light of using the Omicron automated routines so that you will have a better idea of the impact of any given event on volatility in order that you can include consideration of this in your policy for the next time it takes place. Going back over trades is also one of the best ways to get a feel for the market and for price action.

Post activity analysis

Make a routine for studying trades and related matters that have passed. This could happen on those days when no trading can take place because of your policies as delineated in the plan. Do not make it a weekend activity – this identifies it as being of somewhat less importance and, in any event, you need to relax sometime too.

The most important part of making the plan is thinking through the topics here and writing down your decisions on each. Do it!

Chapter Twelve: The Omicron Forex Breakout Strategy

A "random walk" would characterize a price series where all subsequent price changes represent random departures from previous prices.

Burton G. Malkiel: A Random Walk Down Wall Street

Breakouts take place in the here and now

Breakout methods of trading are based on the idea that the market proceeds through time either going up or down (trending) or going sideways without any definable direction (ranging), but that trading opportunities can exist when a move in either direction is initiated. The breakout can take three fundamental forms: the continuation of a trend after an interim flat period, a trend reversal or the ending of a range bound period.

There are many technical indicators that are designed to tell whether or not there is a trend, most of which are based on moving averages. These are calculated, by the computer, by averaging the price from a specified number of time periods, counting back from the current one. As each bar on the chart is filled, the number therefore changes, hence the term moving average. There are simple moving averages (SMAs) and exponential moving averages (EMAs). The latter give greater weight to more recent bar data and are regarded by some as more accurate. Very often the difference between the two will be small. In nearly all cases it is the slope of the curve formed by moving averages that is important, not the absolute value at any given time.

Once again, moving averages can only relate to what has happened in the past. They can give no information about what will happen in the future. They form part of that old bugbear class, lagging indicators.

The Omicron Forex breakout method uses the smallest possible number of technical indicators. Keeping it simple is a very important part of the philosophy. This, in theory at least, means the strategies are ready for anything that happens – predictions are not made, only attempts to go with the direction of the market at any given time.

Market timing

One of the first things you will hear about the Forex market is that it never closes. It is possible, in theory at least, to trade 24 hours a day, seven days a week. However, there are practical constraints on this, both in terms of what is possible and what is desirable. Firstly, most brokers close down their trading servers on weekends. Secondly, the market is dominated by professional traders, who typically work normal office hours. This is true despite what you might hear about the large number that trade from home, and who therefore have access to their systems around the clock. According to a 2004 paper by the academics Galati and Melvin:

"Pension funds, insurance companies, mutual funds and other institutional investors have played an increasingly important role in financial markets in general, and in FX markets in particular, since the early 2000s." (Why has FX trading surged? Explaining the 2004 triennial survey, Galati and Melvin)

The employees of these institutions, together with the people who operate the inter-bank market, which is the most important part of Forex, work office hours. Which hours these are depend on where the office is situated. The most important centres for Forex trading are London and New York. The London market opens at 08:00 local time, which is Greenwich Mean Time (GMT) or GMT + 1 hour depending on daylight saving time and the time of the year that is in question. Five hours later the market opens in NY (except for a brief period every year when daylight saving regimes can overlap).

On a day when no major announcement is to be made, the first hour of trading in these two centres accounts for a very significant proportion of the currency exchange that takes place on any given day. Prices are most likely to move during these times, in one direction or another. For trades involving the Japanese Yen or the Australian Dollar, the opening of the trading desks in the countries that use them takes place around midnight European time, which defines the time of greatest activity in those currencies.

Low volume

Trading outside of regular office hours can also be hazardous due to the fact that, at these times, volume is low. The market is said to be thinly traded, which can give rise to wild swings if some participants place unexpectedly large orders. Wild swings are not what are required. What is desired is an orderly progression of price movement, either up or down through time.

Even on days when an announcement is due, trading can often be vigorous from the open as some participants will have taken a view and will attempt to position themselves in anticipation of being proved correct when the relevant report is released. This happens on the longer time scales as well. You will often hear that an expected change in interest rates has been "priced in" to the exchange rate, a process that can often begin months before the expected change is due to take place. In these cases if what has become the accepted wisdom turns out to be wrong, and it often is, the adverse reaction can be very strong indeed.

Our analysis to date has identified the hours of 08:00 and 13:00 GMT during the summer daylight saving period that runs from 25th March 2012 to 28th October 2012 in London, to be ones when the start of a significant move is most probable. Daylight saving time start and end dates in other countries and in other years are different, and indeed can be quite confusing. However, they must always be factored into both the research and the programming of the setting of trades by automated routines. As 30 minute bars are used by the Omicron Forex breakout strategy for the placing of trades, neglecting daylight saving time could have a profound effect. It is important to understand that price action patterns are constantly in a state of flux and require ongoing examination.

Trade entry

In the Omicron Forex breakout strategy trades are always placed as conditional entry orders. In other words the price has to move, either up or down, to the level at which it has been calculated the trade should be triggered before it will become a live position in the market. As always, a stop loss order is put in place at the same time for each trade.

A trade placed at the close of the 08:00 bar would look like this:

Trade placed by the trading software at the close of the 08:00 bar.

The most noticeable feature is the existence of both a long and a short order, each of which has its associated stop loss instruction.

As it happens, the entry trigger bar above comprises of a classic exhaustion bar, or pin bar, which is giving a signal for a long trade. However, the software does not look for this. If you were to wait for such a setup in each case, trades would be far fewer than they are. Neither would they be guaranteed success. The truth is that no matter what setup is used you are always, but always, playing with probabilities. The risk control and money management techniques are the most important considerations in all cases. For completeness however, a later section of the manual includes details of how the exhaustion bar and other similar bar pattern setups are designed to work.

As mentioned, both a long and a short entry trade have been placed, and each is complete with a stop loss order. The long trade is at the BID and the short trade is at the ASK. This gives a small further advantage over the opposite arrangement, which is what a limit order would entail, because the spread is now in favour of the trader when it comes to deciding the level at which either trade will be triggered. While this advantage might be small, it is important. Remember to think and deal in probability, which is effective only in relation to large numbers of trades. The aggregate value to your account of something like this, along with, for example, being able to calculate prices and place orders to 5 decimal places (one-thousandth of a cent or one-tenth of a pip) can be considerable. Remember that the big players have these facilities, and would find it intolerable to be deprived of them. You want and need to be professional and you do not have to settle for less, as there are brokers out there who facilitate all these things.

While trades may be managed manually if they are filled, and will always be monitored, they are put in place under the control of the trading software. One very important reason for this is the need for precise order placement at a specific time and within a very short time-frame. The sheer difficulty of simultaneously calculating position sizes, stop levels and profit targets for as many as ten orders at the close of a particular bar, using five different Forex pairs (to get the benefits of diversification), and then placing the orders, day in and day out, is something that can only be overcome effectively by a computer.

Trade criteria

The trade placement involves several, carefully researched, elements (or factors in math terms), which are used in the calculations of trade size, stop loss position and target level for the first profit takeoff. In all cases these operate in percentages as opposed to absolute values like numbers of pips (the unit of movement for Forex rates) or specific monetary values. They are exactly the same for both long and short orders.

Long and short orders placed

The arrowed vertical line above, the distance between a possible long and a short order, at present corresponds to 1% of equity. The first target level, calculated and stored in the software routine, also represents 1% of equity. The second vertical line, marked by dots on each end, is the stop loss distance. This represents 0.6% of equity. There is therefore a positive expectation for each trade if it survives beyond the first target, or close to break-even if it falls back (the stop loss will be near or at the trade entry point at that stage). In theory a profit of 0.5% should be made for each trade that reverses immediately after the initial target level is reached. To support the desire for a positive or at least zero expectation it would be preferred to have the stop loss also at 0.5% of equity, but it has been found in practice that this is counterproductive over time, as the trades need the opportunity to work. The difference between 0.6% loss and 0.5% profit actually reflects the cost of the combination of spread and slippage. Again, to be professional, you need to work hard to reduce these as much as possible, by careful broker selection.

The two orders will always be above and below the high or low of the trigger bar on the chart. How much higher or lower has been the focus, again, of research. The optimum value is in a very narrow window. If the gap is too large trades will be filled too late to make profits, and if it is too small too many losses will be incurred as a result of volatility. The results of studies, on years worth of data in both back-testing and real-time trading, are contained in the routines that calculate the entry levels and other criteria. These are then used to work backwards to calculate position size so that the percentages of equity specified above for position size, as it relates to stop loss and first target levels, are always maintained.

The profit level after the first target has been reached is unlimited provided that the progress in our favour does not reverse into the current level of the trailing stop. If the trailing stop is correctly chosen this allows for the continuation of trends, which can be prolonged in Forex.

Managing the trade

After each trade is placed, it must be managed. If it goes into reverse before the first profit is reached, a small loss is incurred. Otherwise, as it goes in the direction of eventual profit, the automated routine begins to operate the trailing stop which moves the stop loss order in the direction of the trade as the rate goes in its favour, with step values that have been determined by research and programmed in. Care has gone into the algorithm that determines the trailing stop step amount. If it is too tight the trade will be terminated prematurely (before full advantage is taken of any trend that develops) while if it is too large it may be found that too much is given back in the event of a reversal.

Definitely not a robot

Forex, and trading in general, might seem straightforward. However, as you are in for the long haul and time is a function of greater uncertainty there is, in fact, much that can go wrong. There is no doubt that at the current state of the art, there are no computer routines that can completely take the place of a human trader. This is unlike the situation in chess, where all but the world's very best Grand Masters will now be defeated repeatedly by an automated chess player. The difference between chess and trading, however, is that the rules of chess are bounded. This means there is a finite number of combinations and permutations of the allowed chess moves. Given sufficient time, computer power, with the use of multiple processors and massive memory, can calculate them all. Forex trading price patterns, on the other hand, are unbounded. Change is constantly taking place, most of it completely unforeseeable. Some of the macro change that has taken place, even recently, like the introduction of the Euro in the 1990s, would be the equivalent of increasing the number of squares on the standard chess board or inventing a new piece with its own unique moves.

At the micro level, the behaviour of institutions and hedge funds is also constantly in a state of flux. The best recent example of this is the growth of High Frequency Trading (HFT). At its most extreme level, this involves computers being programmed to intercept order flow information and placing themselves between the buyer and seller in order to achieve profits that amount to fractions of a cent, but which mount up due to the frequency of the trades. Proponents claim that HFT increases liquidity and reduces spreads, but opponents claim it causes excess volatility.

And then there are the "surprises": everything from unscheduled regulatory announcements to natural disasters, which can come, it might seem, out of a clear blue sky at any time.

Determinism, chaos and human intervention

Problems requiring analysis and resolution that can be assisted by powerful computers include those where the initial conditions and the rules for solution are well defined, even if the work required is onerous. An example of this type is the development of chess playing programs, which are said to fall into the category of being deterministic.

At the other end of the spectrum are those problems where initial conditions have to be chosen by reference to the level of detail that is practicable, and where the circumstances that might be encountered during resolution are imprecise. Weather forecasting by computer falls under this heading. This type of problem has been described as "chaotic".

In all cases the way to proceed is to develop algorithms, or descriptions of the method for solution that proceed in steps that can be coded into a computer language. In both weather forecasting and the playing of chess, this process is now well advanced. These algorithms do not simply search through all possible permutations of chess when deciding on the response to a move from a human opponent or the contents of that day's weather forecast. The designers have incorporated the up-to-date learning about the subject in the algorithm so that a path can be made through the universe of possible solutions without wasting too much time on those that would be trivial or otherwise a waste of time. This is known as a heuristic approach.

The application of algorithms and computer power to electronic trading has been the focus of a lot of activity in recent times. It might be instructive to decide where algorithmic trading sits in the spectrum between the extremes of chaotic conditions on the one hand, and purely deterministic ones on the other. This is important. If "algo" trading tends towards determinism then the only barrier to outright success is the computer power that can be brought to bear on the question.

However, there is another issue. The rules of chess are fixed - all efforts to build a computerised algorithm that can defeat the very best human grand masters proceed on the understanding that the number of pieces and the number and arrangement of the squares on the chess board are fixed, and the moves that are allowed for each piece are unchangeable. Long term suspected changes in climate due to global warming aside, the weather, also, cannot be made subject to human intervention.

But trading can be. As only one example, the practice of stop-hunting is pervasive and well documented. Consider this recent message from the Dow Jones newswire service, on a day when a speech by Mr. Bernanke of the US Federal Reserve was anticipated after an FOMC meeting:

```
DJ MARKET TALK: Euro Drives Toward $1.30
Just Ahead of Bernanke; Algos?

14:21 EDT - Were high-speed traders trying
to trigger stop losses, options before the
Fed chairman starts answering questions?
Whatever the motive, it was a similar
pattern before the Fed statement at 12:30,
when markets moved sharply just
beforehand. This is what algo does to
markets. They move before news, trying to
catch slower players off guard when the
news actually comes out. Healthy? You be
the judge. Bernanke now speaking.
(michael.j.casey@dowjones.com)

(END) Dow Jones Newswires

September 13, 2012 14:21 ET (18:21 GMT)
```

So there is another element that needs to be taken into account – the effects of human intervention in the course of the markets from time to time. This is only one reason why the idea of purchasing a Forex robot that can deliver consistence earnings without supervision is a nonsense, and probably always will be.

But computers are important in Forex trading.

The best way to use automation under current conditions in trading is as an assistant to the human trader. In fact, it has reached the stage where those market participants who do not use it, in a responsible manner, are placing themselves at a disadvantage to those that do. After all, businesses of the smallest size are now well practiced in deploying computers for many functions that would have been done manually in the past, and computer power is also opening up new possibilities for creating competitive advantage, for example in the area of business analysis.

The Omicron Forex routines fall into this category. They are definitely not Forex robots.

Outside of the large institutions, the use of automated strategies is still in its infancy. Like everything else in the start up phase, it is open to exploitation. You will sometimes be offered an automated routine or set of routines that the seller claims is capable of delivering profits on a continuous basis for the foreseeable future. These cannot work. Apart from the market forces that will render such things impractical, you can be sure that if they did work as claimed they would not be offered for sale for a few hundred dollars. The owner would beg, borrow or steal the funds to set up his own account and would make sure to keep the secret very much to himself.

Chapter Thirteen: Price action patterns

"Every action has its pleasures and its price."

Socrates

While the Omicron strategy is based on price action in the sense that it attempts to follow the action that has been initiated by the large institutions, and that can only be defined in terms of price, there is another meaning of price action for trading purposes that is somewhat different. This looks for candlestick bars that conform to certain patterns that are believed by proponents to have predictive powers. This method seems, in particular, to have found favour with many Australian traders.

For completeness and for the avoidance of confusion an example is given here of how the theory works and mention is made of some of the more common price action setups. However, as they are not used for the Omicron Forex breakout trading strategy the treatment here has to be less exhaustive than it otherwise would be.

Candlesticks

One method of recording the movement of prices on a chart is to use candlesticks. They have the benefit of being intuitive. Visually they record a lot of information: the opening and closing prices for the period under review, the highest and lowest price that was attained during the period covered by the bar and whether or not the price went up or down in the same period. There are bars for all the chart periods that can exist, which normally range from as little as one tick, to as high as monthly or even annual periods. The most common charts for the kind of trading Omicron Forex is concerned with are those recording 30-minute, hourly or four hourly bars. Scalpers, or people who attempt to make many small gains on price movement throughout the day might use one-minute or even smaller time charts.

The above illustration shows why they are called candlesticks. Because this bar is coloured black (or red on a colour screen), you know that it opened at the top of the wide, rectangular part (known as the "body") and closed at the bottom of it. During the 30 minutes it took, in this case, to form the bar, it achieved a price as high as the top of the line sticking out upwards. This is known as the bar high. It closed at the bottom so in this case the low price of the bar (bar low) and the bar close price are one and the same.

Pin bars, or exhaustion bars

For the bar above, the following can be inferred: It is coloured white (or green if this book was in colour) so it opened at the bottom of the body and closed at its top. In the meantime it went only very slightly higher than its closing price but went down all the way to the bottom of the line protruding downwards, before coming back up again.

This kind of bar is known as a pin-bar, or exhaustion bar. The idea is the people who were selling, the shorts, could not maintain their downward bias in the face of the actions of those who wanted to buy (the longs). Therefore the downward movement was exhausted, giving rise to the belief that the next and subsequent bars will form in the upward direction. The longs are stronger and the shorts, seeing this, might even be motivated to abandon their belief and join the longs, driving the price up.

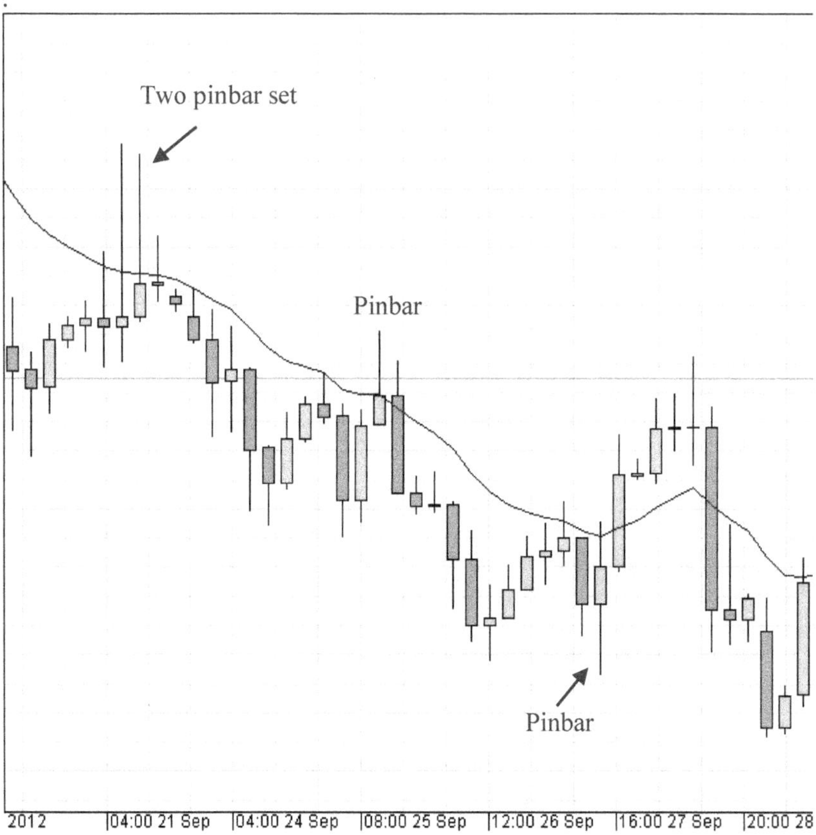

This often seems to work, as in the examples above, which formed on the EUR/USD pair 4-hour chart in September 2012. But by no means always. Here is another example:

Pinbar

As an indicator, this one has the added advantage of pointing to a downward move when prices are already in an obvious downward trend (many traders would use moving averages and other indicators to confirm this).

Here you are looking at “the hard right edge”. You cannot tell until after it happens whether or not the prediction made on the basis of this pinbar, or any other pinbar, will be accurate. You must enter your position with nothing more than hope and expectation.

And this one, in fact, would not have been a good trade. You can see in the next illustration that as time progressed and more information became available, the market turned around and went in the “wrong” direction immediately after the formation of the signal.

The pin bar in the previous illustration, seemingly indicating a downward trade

Many pinbar aficionados have reached the point where they claim to be able to spot those pinbars that point to the opposite of what might seem to be indicated. These have become known as “fake” pinbars and there are methodologies for identifying them. In our opinion all of this only adds to the subjectivity involved.

Other “price action” patterns include inside bars, engulfing patterns, false breakout patterns and one called “Hakkaki” which has its origins in Japan. This is described in an article in Active Trader magazine in April 2004 by Dan Chesler, which also has a useful discussion of the philosophy behind this kind of pattern.

Moving averages

Moving averages are closely allied with price action patterns, as are significant support and resistance levels, where price has failed to advance or fall in the same general area a number of times in the past or where there is a round number price, for example. The idea is that a price action pattern has a better predictive ability if there is a confluence of these events.

As with all other indicators, however, whether or not price will adhere to moving averages is a lottery at best. Consider the following 200 period Exponential Moving Average (EMA) on the 30 minute AUDUSD pair on 30th of August 2012:

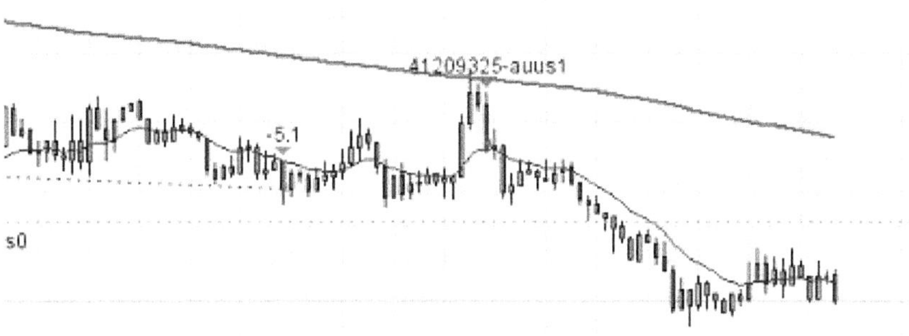

Price rebounds from 200 period EMA

It would be nice to be able to have confidence of when this was going to happen. However, when you look at the same chart setup going back even a short time, you can see that there were other numerous occasions when the price went through the 200 period EMA as if it wasn't there at all:

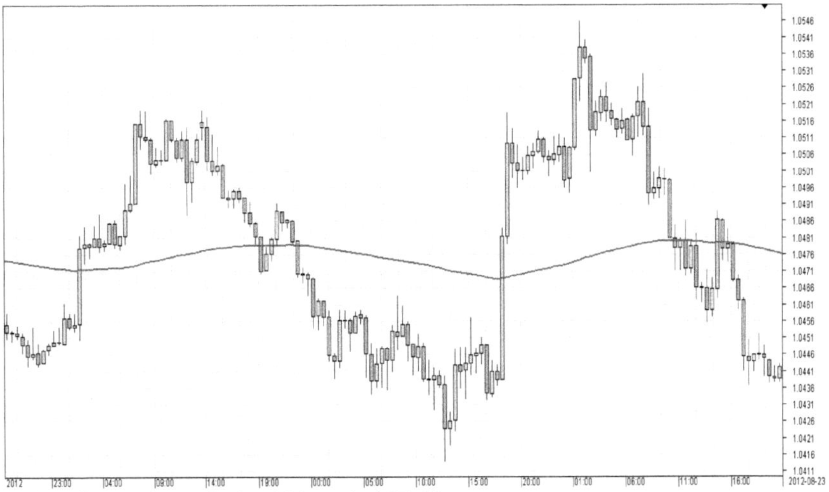

Price slicing through the 200 period EMA

Chapter Fourteen: Installing and running automated strategies

I come in peace," [the silver robot] said, adding after a long moment of further grinding, "take me to your Lizard."

Douglas Adams: The Hitchhiker's Guide to the Galaxy

While the instructions in this section refer to the Dukascopy JForex software "strategies", the procedure for installing "Expert Advisors" in the MetaTrader trading platform are very similar. The purpose of this chapter is to illustrate the ease with which routines can be used in trading. Specific software will always be accompanied by its own instructions for installation and use.

The entire JForex trading platform is written in the Java programming language, which was developed by the Oracle computer company. As a computer programming language it is highly regarded, in widespread use and robust in operation.

Java allows for the development of Application Programming Interfaces (APIs). These are specialised routines where necessary underlying functionality has already been programmed in. As an example, by using the Dukascopy Java API included with the JForex trading platform, placing a trade will be taken care of by a sub-routine that is called by the programmer who wishes to carry out such an action, without having to "re-invent the wheel" every time.

The Dukascopy JForex Java API has been used to build the Omicron Forex automated routines. When compiled, these are free-standing programs that the trading platform expects to find in one of its dedicated folders called, appropriately enough, the "Strategies" folder.

To begin using the automated strategies, you must have access to the JForex platform. You can do that by going to any of the following brokers:

www.dukascopy.com

www.alpari.com

www.fxdd.com

and opening a demo account in the first instance. You can open a live account later. You must specify that you need your trading to be carried out using the JForex trading platform. There will be others available but they will not be able to run the JForex strategies.

When the platform is installed, which will happen automatically every time you log on to your broker trading account, you must install the JForex strategies.

When you download a JForex strategy, you should do so by right-clicking on the download link and choosing "Save target as"

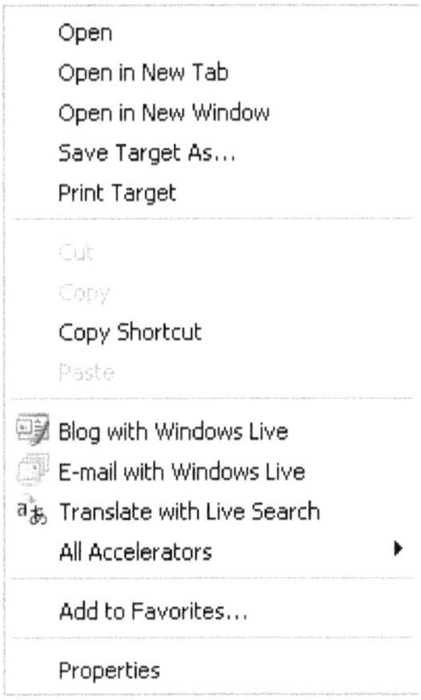

Then navigate to the JForex strategies folder:

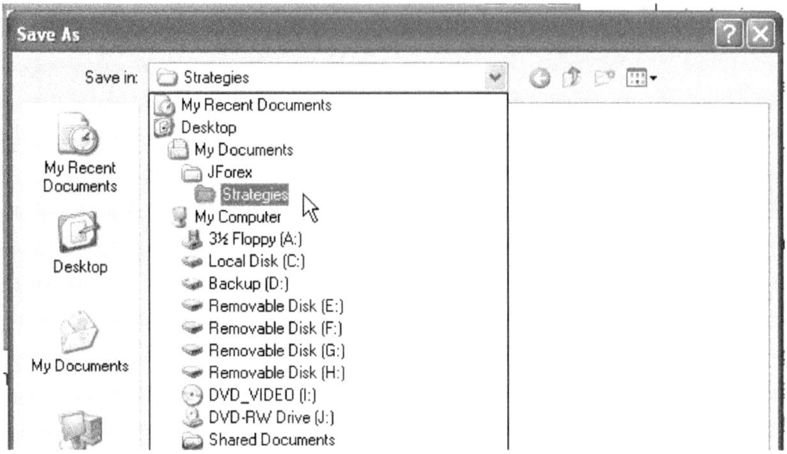

Which you will find in the path: My Documents > JForex > Strategies

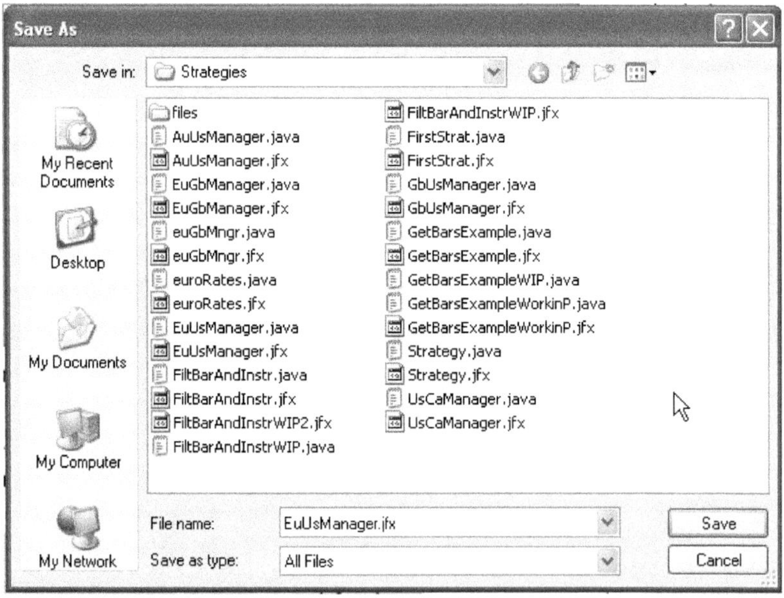

Hit "Save" and you are done as far as downloading and storing the strategy is concerned.

You can use the strategies you have stored in a number of places in the JForex platform: If you want to see it in action in real-time, then make it visible by right clicking on the strategies area in the workspace part of the JForex platform, choosing "Open strategy" and then picking the one you want.

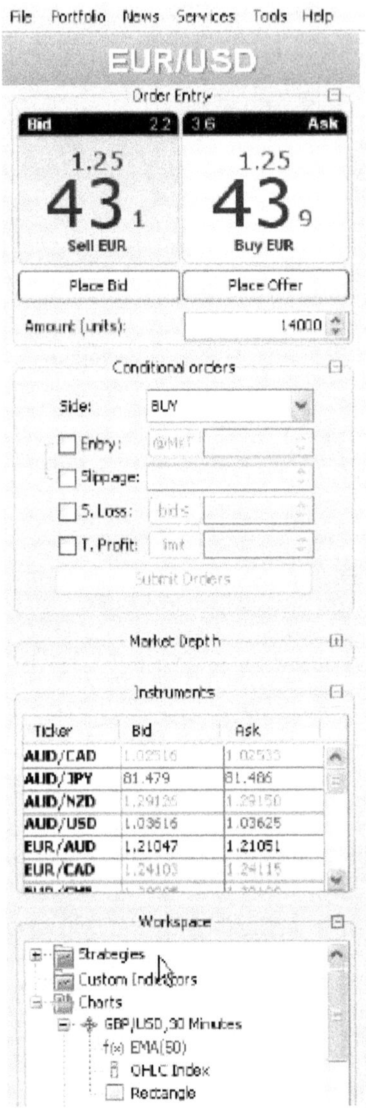
File Portfolio News Services Tools Help
EUR/USD
Order Entry
Bid 2.2
3.6 Ask
1.25 43 1
1.25 43 9
Sell EUR
Buy EUR
Place Bid
Place Offer
Amount (units): 14000
Conditional orders
Side: BUY
Entry: @MKT
Slippage:
S. Loss:
T. Profit:
Submit Orders
Market Depth
Instruments
Ticker Bid Ask
AUD/CAD
AUD/JPY 81.479 81.486
AUD/NZD
AUD/USD 1.03616 1.03625
EUR/AUD 1.21047 1.21051
EUR/CAD
Workspace
Strategies
Custom Indicators
Charts
GBP/USD,30 Minutes
f(x) EMA(50)
OHLC Index
Rectangle

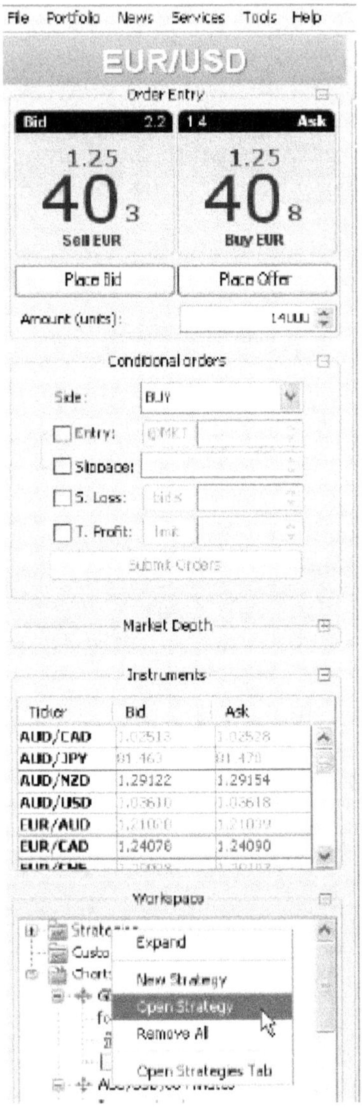
File Portfolio News Services Tools Help
EUR/USD
Order Entry
Bid 2.2
1.4 Ask
1.25 40 3
1.25 40 8
Sell EUR
Buy EUR
Place Bid
Place Offer
Amount (units): 14000
Conditional orders
Side: BUY
Entry: @MKT
Slippage:
S. Loss:
T. Profit:
Submit Orders
Market Depth
Instruments
Ticker Bid Ask
AUD/CAD
AUD/JPY
AUD/NZD 1.29122 1.29154
AUD/USD
EUR/AUD
EUR/CAD 1.24076 1.24090
Workspace
Expand
New Strategy
Open Strategy
Remove All
Open Strategies Tab

When that is done just right click once more on the strategy itself and choose “Local Run”.

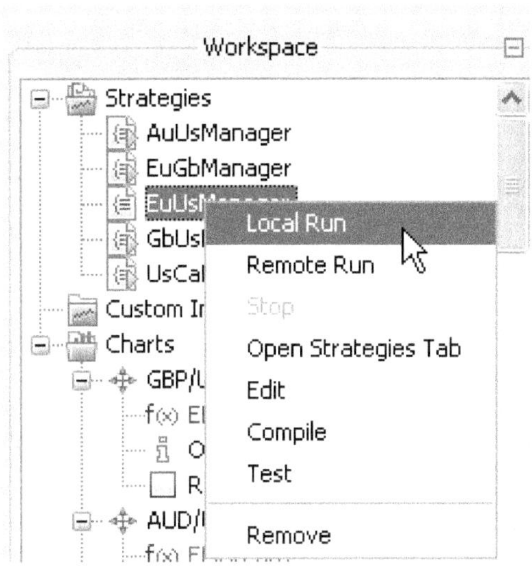

That is it. The trading platform is now under the control of the Omicron Forex automated routine. You will not find it very exciting, however, especially at the start and if you have activated it some time before the trigger 30-minute bar.

For more action, you can use the strategy in the Historical Tester. You do not need to do any additional configuration for this. Simply open the Historical Tester, choose the strategy, set the instruments (currency pairs) to be tested, the time period over which you wish to test and hit the Start button. You should also make sure that the “Visual mode” box is ticked, although this will probably be the case by default. If nothing happens it is probably because you have not chosen the correct pairs, or the “Visual mode” box has been cleared.

If the Historical Tester is not visible in the platform, you can invoke it by choosing “Historical Tester” under “Tools”:

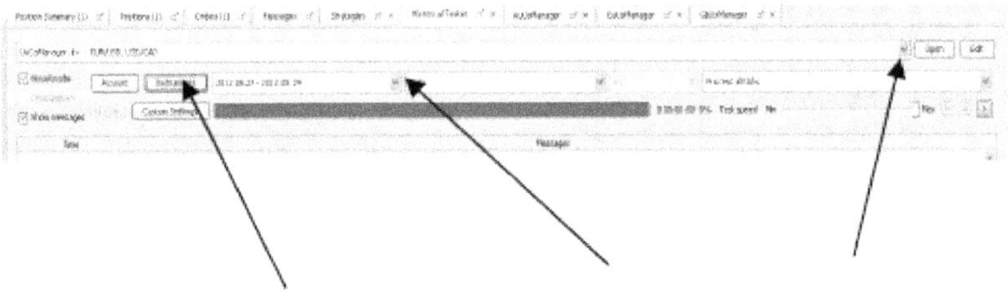

Choose instruments

Dropdown to choose the period

Dropdown to choose the strategy to run

The Historical Tester.

Choosing pairs in the Historical Tester

When running a strategy in the tester it might be necessary to choose two pairs under “Instruments”. This will occur when you are testing a pair where the base currency (the first one to be quoted in the pair) is not your home currency. Thus, if your home currency (the currency that your account is denominated in) is, say, USD, and you wish to test EUR/AUD, you will need to choose both EUR/AUD (the pair to be tested) and EUR/USD (for the conversion of the base (EUR) into your home currency). If you wanted to test USD/CAD you would only need to choose that pair, as the base currency of the pair is also your home unit.

Avoid using the "Select All" button as this will cause confusion, especially if you have ticked the Visual Mode box.

Conclusion

It ain't over till it's over

American colloquialism

There are many approaches to trading Foreign Exchange but they all boil down to having a methodology, a concentration on capital retention and the mindset that allows you to see the big picture both on those occasions when it seems you can do no wrong, and at those other times when the market is effectively telling you to keep away.

That things will change over time is one of the few certainties in trading. There was a time when options, for example, were poorly priced so that option traders who were aware could garner a strong advantage for themselves. This did not last long and today the advantage is once again very much on the side of the intermediaries in the options game. The balance between intrinsic value and time value is skewed and in the meantime, the clock just keeps on ticking.

Forex is effectively the new kid on the block. It is only in relatively recent times that the ability to trade currency pairs was made available to retail traders. As you will be aware if you have read the foregoing, the advantages that Forex enjoys for small traders have a lot to do with the fact that it is not totally a secondary market, such as is the case with almost all derivatives and even, in many cases, the common stock of quoted corporations.

Another area of change is in relation to the use of computers. The brokers have been taking advantage of technology to enable dealing as well as to keep records for a long time now. So have retail traders, but only insofar as maintaining a front-end, or client system, attached to the broker's server for the purpose of placing orders. The big change is in the use of computers by traders so that they can decide when to place orders and, then, for the management of those orders. As pointed out elsewhere, computers also have a big part to play in educating traders. The use of an Historical Tester is very effective in demonstrating the importance of thinking in probabilities, and in determining what constitute the most important elements of your trading strategy.

Change is the only constant

Trading strategies have changed. Not so long ago the emphasis was on stochastics, MACD graphs and all sorts of other indicators. The new focus seems to be on so-called price action, involving pin bars, outside and inside bars and the Hakkiki pattern, among others. All very fine, but at the end of the day these too are indicators that can only be constructed on the basis of price movement that has taken place in the past. For this and other reasons they are far from infallible. The question still comes down to one of ensuring, on those occasions when the trade goes your way, that its benefits in terms of profitability will be maximised and its losses, should it go the other way, be cut off at the optimum point.

And that is where the most important elements enter in. A well designed trailing stop is more important than any indicator. Its design requires the analysis of many months and years of price movement, and that mandates the use of a computer and an algorithm. Once designed, the trailing stop can only be implemented properly by a computer. Sitting in front of your screen and trying to judge when and how far to move your stop loss is a tedious occupation. When this has to be simultaneously applied to many different pairs (to get the benefits of diversification) it also becomes prone to error, as does the placing of the orders itself.

It is hoped you will investigate this and other related questions a bit more. To see what Dukascopy are doing about the matter, go to the Dukascopy - Code Editor at:

https://www.dukascopy.com/wiki/en/manuals/jforex4-desktop/editor/

Bibliography

Arvedlund, Erin	Madoff: The man who stole $65 Billion	London	Penquin	2009
Bing, Stanley	Sun Zsu Was A Sissy	New York:	Harper Business	2004
Covey, Stephen R.	The 7 Habits of Highly Effective People	London	Simon & Schuster	1989
Dalton, Jones and Dalton	Mind over Markets	Greenville, SC	Traders Press Inc	1993
Douglas, Mark	Trading in the Zone	New York:	Prentice Hall	2000
Douglas, Mark	The Disciplined Trader	New York:	Prentice Hall	1990
Elder, Dr. Alexander	Trading for a Living	New York:	John Wiley & Sons	1993
Elder, Dr. Alexander	Come into my Trading Room	New York:	John Wiley & Sons	2002

Francis, Jack Clark	Investments, Analysis and Management	New York:	McGraw-Hill	1986
Galbraith, John Kenneth	The Great Crash 1929	London	Alan Lane	1954
Douglas, Mark	The age of Uncertainty	London	André Deutsch	1977
Lefevre, Edwin	* Reminiscences Of A Stock Operator	New York:	John Wiley & Sons	1993
Link, Marcel	High Probability Trading	New York:	McGraw-Hill	2003
Malkiel, Burton G.	A Random Walk Down Wall Street	New York:	WW Norton & Co.	1996
Miner, Robert C.	High Probability Trading Strategies	New York:	John Wiley & Sons	2009

* Originally published in 1923 by George H. Doran and Company

Peters, Tom and Waterman, Robert.	In Search of Excellence	New York:	Harper and Row,	1982
Seife, Charles	Zero, the biography of a dangerous idea	London	Souvenir Press	2000
Smith, Courtney D.	Trading Foreign Exchange	New York:	John Wiley & Sons	2010

www.ingramcontent.com/pod-product-compliance
Lightning Source LLC
LaVergne TN
LVHW050820061126
851857LV00012B/896
* 9 7 8 1 0 6 8 4 3 0 6 2 6 *